The Book of Giants

A Restored Apocryphal Account of the Watchers' Rebellion, the Nephilim's Rise, and Enoch's Prophetic Role

Rush Nilson

Manuscryptha©Copyright 2025

All rights reserved.

Protected with www.protectmywork.com,

The material within this book may not be copied, reproduced, or shared in any form without explicit written permission from the author or publisher.

Under no circumstances shall the author or publisher be held liable for any damages, financial losses, or other consequences resulting directly or indirectly from the information provided in this book.

Legal Notice:

This book is protected by copyright and is intended for personal use only. You may not modify, distribute, sell, quote, or reproduce any portion of its content without prior consent from the author or publisher.

Disclaimer:

The content in this book is meant solely for educational and entertainment purposes. Every effort has been made to ensure that the information is accurate, current, and reliable. However, no guarantees or warranties, either expressed or implied, are provided.

Readers acknowledge that the author is not offering legal, financial, medical, or professional advice. The content is derived from various sources, and it is strongly recommended to consult a licensed professional before attempting any methods outlined in this book.

By reading this material, you agree that the author is not responsible for any direct or indirect losses resulting from the use of the information contained within, including errors, omissions, or inaccuracies.

TABLE OF CONTENTS

INTRODUCTION	**1**
CHAPTER 1	**2**
Prologue	2
The Return of the Giants	3
CHAPTER 2	**7**
Discovery and Fragments: The Lost Pages of Humanity	7
CHAPTER 3	**13**
A Tale of Angels and Giants: Myth or Cosmic History?	13
CHAPTER 4	**19**
Versions and Sources	19
Method od Textual Reconstruction	23
CHAPTER 5	**25**
Structure of this edition: a Unique Layout	25
CHAPTER 6	**29**
Enoch, the scribe of heaven	29
1. Origin of the Giants	35
2. Narrative Structure	35
3. Role of Enoch	36
4. Dreams and Visions	37
5. Divine Judgment	38
6. Silence of Heaven	39
CHAPTER 7	**42**
Themes and Symbols: Dreams, Judgment, Rebellion	42
CHAPTER 8	**48**
Why this book still matters	48
CHAPTER 9	**53**
Invitation to the Mystery	53

THE BOOK OF GIANTS — 58
Parallel Text – Fragments and Interpretive Paraphrase — 58
Closing Note – End of the Record — 83

APPENDIX 1
ENOCH, THE CELESTIAL MEDIATOR — 85
Between Worlds: The Role of the Celestial Scribe — 85
The Heavenly Ascent: Enoch's Transformation — 87
A Voice of Judgment: Enoch and the Watchers — 89
Enoch and Divine Knowledge: Secrets and Silence — 92
From Man to Metatron: The Evolution of Enoch in Later Traditions — 94
Mediator of Justice and Mercy: Enoch's Enduring Symbolism — 97

APPENDIX 2
CONNECTIONS WITH OTHER APOCRYPHAL TEXTS — 100
Voices Across the Texts — 100
The Book of Watchers (1 Enoch 6–36) — 101
The Book of Jubilees — 104
Genesis Apocryphon (1Q20) — 107
The Second Book of Enoch (2 Enoch) — 110
Gnostic Echoes: Gospel of Judas & Gospel of Mary — 113
A Myth That Endures — 116

INTRODUCTION

CHAPTER 1

Prologue

This edition of The Book of Giants is based on a critical comparison between the Aramaic fragments discovered among the Dead Sea Scrolls and the Manichaean versions in Middle Persian, preserved primarily in Central Asian literature. The Aramaic fragments, dating back to the 2nd century BCE, represent the earliest known version of the text and are closely linked to the Enochic tradition. The Manichaean texts, though later, offer complementary insights valuable for narrative and thematic reconstruction.

The selection and presentation of the fragments in this edition follow both philological and symbolic-narrative criteria. Where the Aramaic text is too fragmented, interpretive paraphrases inspired by parallel sources and broader apocryphal traditions have been used. Each fragment is accompanied by a narrative paraphrase that offers one possible reading—without claiming to replace the original—but aiming to make its deeper meaning accessible.

The terminology used aligns with classic translations of 1 Enoch, while respecting the stylistic distinctiveness of the Giants text. Particular attention has been given to the role of Enoch as celestial scribe and divine messenger—a key figure in conveying judgment and mediating between the angelic realm and humanity.

CHAPTER 1

The Return of the Giants

There are stories that never truly disappear. Buried beneath sand and silence, hidden in broken scrolls and ancient whispers, they wait—patiently. The Book of Giants is one of these stories. Its fragments, scattered across centuries and continents, speak of a time before time, of beings neither wholly divine nor entirely mortal, and of a world teetering between cosmic order and chaos.

Long before the flood, before the tower, before the prophets, there was a rebellion. Not of men, but of Watchers—celestial beings who descended from the heights to dwell among mortals. What followed was not a tale of peace. It was transgression. From their union with human women came the Nephilim: giants of immense power, fierce in appetite, corrupted in purpose. Their presence spread like wildfire across the early earth, bringing knowledge and ruin, enlightenment and destruction.

These were not simple myths passed down around tribal fires. They were encoded into the sacred memory of ancient cultures—echoes of something terrifyingly real. We find their shadows in Genesis 6, in the scrolls of Qumran, in the dreams of Enoch, and in the banned pages of forgotten apocalypses. Their story was told and retold, then censored, erased, or sealed away. And yet, it remained.

In hidden corners of the apocryphal tradition, this story quietly endured. Texts outside the official canon carried its embers forward. The *Book of Jubilees*, a "Little Genesis" preserved by ancient communities, retold the descent of the Watchers and the birth of the giants in painstaking detail—ensuring that the sin of the angels and the flood that cleansed it would not be forgotten. In another vision, known as *4 Ezra*, a prophet grieving the fall of Jerusalem questions why evil was ever allowed to flourish; the answers he receives echo the very themes of the Giants' saga: a rebellion against Heaven's law and the sorrowful necessity of divine judgment. Even as authorities tried to bury the tale, these forbidden scriptures kept it alive, passing the torch of memory from one secret reader to the next.

The Book of Giants, in its surviving form, is not a complete narrative. What we have are shards—pieces of a cosmic drama once known across vast stretches of the ancient world. The fragments speak in multiple voices: some from the scrolls found near the Dead Sea, others from remote deserts of Central Asia, preserved within the teachings of later mystical sects. And though broken, the pieces still burn with urgency. They tell of fallen angels and their monstrous offspring, of dreams that foretold doom, of divine messengers delivering judgment, and of a man—Enoch—chosen to bear witness and record it all.

To read the Book of Giants today is not merely to explore an ancient curiosity. It is to confront one of the earliest attempts to explain evil, power, and rebellion in spiritual terms. These stories ask—not with sentiment but with severity—what happens when heavenly boundaries are crossed. What is the cost of divine knowledge misused? What happens to a world when the sacred order is violated?

And yet, within this tale of ruin, there is also a hidden yearning: a longing for restoration, for justice, for the return of divine harmony. Enoch, who walks among angels and speaks to those beyond the veil, becomes a symbol—not of wrath, but of mediation. His role is not to conquer, but to record; not to destroy, but to warn. He is the bridge between realms, the voice that speaks truth into chaos.

Now, after centuries of silence, the Book of Giants returns—not in the fullness it once had, but in fragments that still pulse with significance. These texts are more than relics. They are keys. Keys to understanding how ancient minds grappled with the presence of evil, with the mystery of corrupted wisdom, and with the terrifying beauty of the divine.

In this edition, the reader is invited to move between two layers: the ancient text in its restored form, and a contemporary paraphrase that seeks to make its message clearer without losing its gravity. Each line carries the weight of a world long vanished but never irrelevant.

The giants may have fallen, but their story still rises.

CHAPTER 2

Discovery and Fragments: The Lost Pages of Humanity

The Book of Giants, as we know it today, does not come to us whole. It exists in pieces—like a shattered mirror once reflecting a great cosmic story. These fragments, recovered across more than a century of discoveries, are among the most tantalizing and mysterious remnants of ancient spiritual thought. They speak of rebellion in heaven, the birth of giants on earth, and a judgment that fell upon both. But before we can read their words, we must first understand how they survived at all.

The first major traces of the Book of Giants were uncovered in the mid-20th century among the scrolls found near the Dead Sea. These were not just any scrolls. Hidden in caves near Qumran, they had rested in silence for almost two thousand years. When archaeologists and Bedouin shepherds unearthed them, they revealed a world of ancient writings once thought lost—texts from the Essene community, apocalyptic visions, and writings once considered sacred by fringe Jewish groups. Among these treasures were scraps of Aramaic parchment: faded, damaged, but unmistakable in their references to Watchers, giants, and Enoch.

Remarkably, those caves held not just the fragmented *Book of Giants* itself, but companion accounts that shed light on its tale. The very library of Qumran included the *Book of Jubilees*, which boldly expands Genesis by describing how the Watchers descended and how their giant offspring brought chaos—offering a parallel chronicle to the Giants' story within a scriptural framework. Another manuscript from Qumran, the *Genesis Apocryphon*, records a patriarch's astonishment at the birth of a glowing child (the infant Noah) and whispers that heavenly beings might be the fathers of such giants. The Essenes who kept these scrolls clearly knew of the Watchers' transgression from multiple sources. In their desert sanctuary, the tale of the giants was not a single, isolated narrative but part of a wider tapestry of forbidden history that they guarded and pondered.

The Qumran fragments include several manuscripts: 1Q23, 1Q24, 2Q26, and a group collectively known as 4Q531–4Q533. Each bears bits and pieces of what scholars now identify as the Book of Giants. Though many lines are missing or barely legible, certain names and phrases repeat: Mahway, Ohyah, Hahyah, Shemihaza, Virōgdād. These names—strange, often non-Hebrew in sound—appear consistently in the various manuscripts, giving structure to an otherwise fragmented narrative.

Most of these pieces are written in Aramaic, the everyday language of Jews in the Second Temple period. This is significant. Aramaic was not the liturgical language of the Torah—it was the language of stories told outside the mainstream. The Book of Giants did not belong to temple priests or court scribes. It

CHAPTER 2

belonged to visionaries, mystics, and apocalyptic thinkers on the edges of tradition.

But Qumran was not the only place where echoes of this book appeared. In the late 19th and early 20th centuries, missionaries and explorers traveling in Central Asia uncovered strange and unfamiliar texts in caves near Turfan and Dunhuang, regions once touched by the ancient Silk Road. These texts were written in languages like Sogdian, Parthian, and Middle Persian—languages of ancient Iranian peoples—and were part of the literature of Manichaeism, a powerful spiritual movement founded by Mani in the 3rd century CE.

Mani, who claimed to be the final prophet in a long chain that included Enoch, Jesus, and Zoroaster, adopted the Book of Giants into his own sacred canon. He gave the story new life in a different religious framework—one shaped by cosmic dualism, light and darkness, soul and matter. In Manichaean texts, the giants become beings of chaos born from the union of demons and women, sent to sow destruction in the material world. Enoch, called the apostle, brings messages of judgment to the fallen angels and their children. In these retellings, we glimpse both fidelity to the original vision and layers of theological reinterpretation.

Some of the most evocative passages from the Manichaean Book of Giants survive only in translation—from Aramaic to Middle Persian, from Sogdian to Chinese, then back again into modern languages. And yet, the spirit of the story remains clear. The names, the visions, the warnings—they speak with the same urgency.

What is remarkable is how similar the Aramaic and Manichaean versions are at their core. Despite the difference in cultures and centuries, they describe the same cast of characters, the same dreams of doom, the same divine intervention. In both, we find a world in crisis, corrupted by heavenly beings who crossed forbidden boundaries, and by their offspring who brought violence, greed, and chaos to the earth.

This consistency across languages, geographies, and religious systems suggests something important: the story of the giants was never a minor tale. It had weight. It circulated widely. It spoke to something deep in the ancient imagination—a fear of hybrid power, a warning about the misuse of knowledge, and a longing for cosmic justice.

Today, the surviving fragments allow us to reconstruct much of the original story. Through comparison of Aramaic scrolls, Manichaean texts, and references in other apocryphal writings, scholars have begun to piece together a coherent narrative. It begins with the descent of the Watchers, their oath of rebellion, and their descent to earth. It continues with the birth of the giants, the chaos they unleash, the prophetic dreams that foresee their doom, and the arrival of Enoch, who delivers a message of judgment and warns of the coming flood.

But we must be clear: the Book of Giants is not a "lost book" in the romantic sense. It was silenced. Censored. Excluded. Its ideas were too dangerous, too strange, or too unorthodox for the religious systems that triumphed. And yet it survived—not because of institutional preservation, but because of its enduring resonance. It touched something primal.

As readers of these ancient fragments, we are not merely observers. We are participants in a rediscovery. We are gathering the scattered pieces of a sacred story that once crossed mountains, deserts, and empires. A story that was told in Aramaic by desert scribes, retold in Persian by mystics, preserved by accident and obsession, and now made whole—imperfectly, but faithfully—in your hands.

The pages ahead do not offer a complete scripture. They offer something else: a bridge between worlds. Between the seen and the unseen, the ancient and the now. The Book of Giants is not just a story. It is a return.

CHAPTER 3

A Tale of Angels and Giants: Myth or Cosmic History?

In the beginning, the heavens were silent. The celestial order moved with purpose, untouched by desire or rebellion. But then came the descent. A group of divine beings, known as the Watchers, chose to leave their appointed realm. They descended not out of accident, but intention—drawn by the beauty of the daughters of men.

This act marked the first fracture. These angels, once pure and bound to heavenly law, swore an oath together atop Mount Hermon. That place became cursed by their promise. From this forbidden union came a new generation: the giants. Colossal in stature and insatiable in hunger, they walked the earth like storms made flesh. Their names—Ohyah, Mahway, Hahyah, Gilgamesh—echo with weight. They were not only powerful but born of heaven and earth, distorted in spirit, unpredictable in form.

The giants became the scourge of the ancient world. They consumed everything in their path—not only animals, but also humans. And when food ran out, they turned on each other. Their violence was not just physical. With the knowledge inherited from their angelic fathers, they brought corrupted wisdom to humanity. Sorcery, enchantments, astrology, forbidden arts—what was once divine became twisted through their touch.

The world groaned under their weight. Blood filled the rivers. The cries of the oppressed rose to the heavens. Even the earth itself, ancient and vast, could no longer bear their corruption. It was then that the dreams began.

The giants, for all their arrogance, were haunted by visions. Mahway dreamed of a tablet thrown into water, dissolving in waves. Only three names remained. Ohyah saw trees uprooted by a great flood. Hahyah spoke of fire and wings, of messengers of judgment descending from the sky. These dreams unsettled them. They could not interpret what they had seen. The meaning eluded them—perhaps because, in their hearts, they already knew it.

In desperation, Mahway flew—either literally or in spirit—to the ends of the earth to seek answers. He crossed boundaries forbidden even to angels. There, beyond the mortal plane, he found Enoch.

Enoch was unlike other men. Born of flesh but not bound by it, he had been taken into the heavens, clothed in knowledge, and appointed as scribe of the Most High. He walked among stars. He spoke with the holy ones. He wrote the decrees of judgment and mercy. To Mahway and his kin, Enoch was their last hope.

They begged him to intercede. They asked him to explain the meaning of the dreams. But Enoch did not offer comfort. His vision was clear, and it was final. The union of heaven and earth was an abomination. The giants, born of unnatural origin, would face annihilation. Their fathers—the Watchers—would be bound and cast into the depths, awaiting their final judgment. Their children—the giants—would perish before the face of the flood.

The dreams were not warnings. They were confirmations.

Enoch's message to the Watchers was delivered with solemnity: You shall have no peace. Their sin was not ignorance, but willful rebellion. They had crossed divine boundaries, not just once, but with full knowledge and consent. They had brought suffering to a world not meant to carry such weight. And now, the flood would come—not just as water, but as cleansing fire from the sky, as silence from the deep, as a final rewriting of corrupted lines.

The tale of the giants is more than myth. It holds within it a reflection of deep patterns: the consequences of rebellion, the danger of corrupted power, the weight of divine justice. It is a story found not only in the Book of Giants, but mirrored across cultures and ages. The Nephilim of Genesis, the titans of Greece, the Asuras of India, the Anunnaki of Mesopotamia—all speak to an ancient memory, shared and reshaped through generations.

Across the world's mythologies, the pattern repeats with uncanny similarity. In Greek lore, the primeval Titans—giants in their own right—once rebelled against the Olympian gods and were cast down into Tartarus, imprisoned beneath the earth for their transgressions. In the far North, Norse sagas tell of the Jötnar, a race of giants who emerged at creation's dawn;

they perpetually clash with the gods and are fated to storm the heavens during Ragnarök, nearly bringing the cosmos to ruin in a final battle of fire and flood. Ancient Mesopotamian tablets speak of monstrous forces of chaos, like the hulking offspring of Tiamat, defeated only by the courage of Marduk to restore order. Each culture told and retold its version of a war between heaven and its own children—a cycle of hubris and retribution. Even within the Book of Giants itself, we find evidence of this shared memory: among the names of the Watchers' offspring appears **Gilgamesh**, the legendary hero-king of Sumerian epics, here reimagined as one of the doomed giants. Such an unexpected cameo is a tantalizing hint that these stories were crossing borders and intertwining. The ancient audience, hearing *Gilgamesh* alongside *Ohyah* and *Mahway*, would have realized that the tale they read was part of something larger. The drama of proud giants and divine judgment was not confined to one people or scripture—it was a truth their neighbors knew as well, spoken in different tongues and given different names, yet echoing the same fear and hope.

Yet here, in this fragmented tale, there is a particular gravity. The giants are not mere brutes. They are tragic beings, caught between dimensions, heirs to both glory and doom. They do not seek evil for its own sake, but act from pride, confusion, and a longing to belong somewhere—heaven or earth. Their very existence challenges the balance of creation.

The Book of Giants does not offer easy answers. It doesn't draw neat lines between good and evil, between man and angel.

Instead, it presents a world where boundaries matter, where power has consequence, and where justice, though delayed, is never absent.

In the center of this tale stands Enoch—not as a warrior, but as a witness. He does not fight with weapons, but with words. His role is not to destroy, but to declare. He sees, he listens, he writes. He speaks not for his own glory, but as a bridge between realms that were never meant to cross

This is a story of tension: between heaven and earth, desire and obedience, knowledge and restraint. It is a story that moves from chaos to cleansing, from broken order to divine intervention. And though much of the Book of Giants has been lost, what remains still resonates. The voices of the Watchers, the cries of the oppressed, the dreams of destruction—they continue to echo, waiting to be heard again.

CHAPTER 4

Versions and Sources

The Book of Giants, as preserved today, exists only in fragments—but these fragments speak in many tongues. The story has traveled across languages, regions, and religious traditions. Each version offers its own perspective, shaped by the beliefs and conditions of the community that transmitted it. While the core narrative remains recognizable, the variations reveal how widespread and influential the myth of the giants truly was.

The earliest known texts are in Aramaic, discovered among the Dead Sea Scrolls at Qumran. These fragments are believed to date from the 2nd century BCE and are written in the same script as other apocalyptic and pseudepigraphal texts. Their language, imagery, and theology place them within the world of Second Temple Judaism, alongside works like 1 Enoch, Jubilees, and the Book of the Watchers. These scrolls reflect a worldview shaped by cosmic conflict, angelic rebellion, and divine justice.

The Aramaic version is fragmented and often difficult to interpret. Many lines are missing or barely legible. Still, it is clear that this was not a standalone book, but part of a larger body of literature centered on Enoch. In this context, the Book of Giants appears to serve as a kind of dramatic prelude to the flood narrative—a missing chapter that explains why divine judgment became inevitable. The central characters—Mahway, Ohyah, Hahyah, and others—appear consistently in the Aramaic scrolls, suggesting that these names and figures were well known within the tradition. The names themselves, often of non-Semitic origin, point to a diverse cultural background. Some may be echoes of Mesopotamian figures, others of Iranian or even older oral traditions. This hybrid quality gives the text a mythic depth that transcends any one culture. Centuries later, the story reappears in an entirely different form within the literature of Manichaeism. Founded in the 3rd century CE by the prophet Mani, this syncretic religion blended elements of Christianity, Zoroastrianism, and Buddhism. Mani viewed himself as a successor to Enoch and incorporated the Book of Giants into his sacred writings. The result was a retelling of the story in Middle Persian, Parthian, Sogdian, and even Chinese.

In the Manichaean version, the giants become demonic entities—beings of chaos and material corruption. Their fathers, the Watchers, are portrayed as rebellious spirits who attempt to drag divine light into the prison of matter. Enoch is no longer just a messenger, but a cosmic prophet who brings warnings to the fallen angels and announces their ultimate defeat. The focus shifts from historical judgment to metaphysical warfare between light and darkness.

Though the theology is different, the narrative framework remains strikingly similar. The names are often preserved. The dreams of doom, the efforts to reach Enoch, the divine response—all appear again, reinterpreted for a new spiritual vision. The Manichaean texts confirm that the Book of Giants was not a marginal legend, but a powerful myth capable of crossing boundaries—linguistic, geographical, and religious.

A third witness to the Book of Giants comes from the Greek world. Though no complete Greek manuscript has survived, early Christian writers allude to it. Tertullian, for example, mentions a "scripture of Enoch" that spoke of the judgment upon the angels and the birth of monstrous offspring. Later quotations, some of which reflect Greek idioms and vocabulary, suggest that the Book of Giants may have circulated in a Hellenized form, either as part of 1 Enoch or as an independent narrative.

Indeed, the influence of this saga even crept into early Christian thought. The New Testament itself contains a subtle homage: in the Epistle of Jude, Enoch's prophecy against the Watchers is quoted, affirming that the fallen angels are bound for judgment. Church fathers like Clement of Alexandria and Origen read these words and took them seriously, openly pondering the reality of the "sons of God" from Genesis and their giant offspring. Some, like Tertullian, argued fervently that believers should not shun the *Book of Enoch* (and by extension the stories akin to the Book of Giants) just because it lay outside the Hebrew canon. While the Book of Giants did not become part of official scripture, its themes seeped through the cracks—into sermons, letters, and apocalyptic visions—ensuring that the memory of the Watchers' transgression and its punishment echoed through the early churches in fragmentary, yet persistent, whispers.

In modern scholarship, these versions are studied side by side. The Aramaic fragments are considered the oldest and most directly tied to Jewish tradition. The Manichaean texts show how the story evolved in a dualistic framework, emphasizing spiritual conflict. The possible Greek traces suggest that the legend may have influenced early Christian apocalyptic thought as well.

What emerges is not a single book, but a web of texts, interpretations, and adaptations. The Book of Giants is less a fixed canon than a living myth, reshaped by each culture that received it. Yet through all these transformations, the core remains: a rebellion in heaven, the birth of the giants, their violence and despair, the prophetic visions of judgment, and the mediating role of Enoch.

The version included in this edition is based on the Hellenistic tradition, reconstructed and translated from known fragments, parallels, and early references. While not complete, it presents the most cohesive narrative structure available. This version offers a glimpse into what the story might have looked like when it was still told aloud, passed from voice to voice in times of fear, wonder, and longing for justice. It is important to remember that each version is a lens. Aramaic, Greek, Persian—they do not compete, but complement. Together, they help reveal the depth and reach of a tradition that refused to be forgotten. The Book of Giants is not just a document. It is a survival. A sacred ruin whose echoes have crossed centuries to speak again.

CHAPTER 4

Method od Textual Reconstruction

The reconstruction process adopted in this edition follows a dual approach: first, fidelity to the fragment order proposed by leading scholars (Milik, Reeves, García Martínez); second, a coherent narrative restoration that provides a meaningful reading experience even for non-specialist audiences.

During this process, distinctions were carefully maintained between original lines, textual gaps, and interpretive additions. Each fragment is presented in its essential form, with minimal supplementation where meaning can be recovered through context or parallel literature. The paraphrases are not intended to replace the original but serve as a narrative guide supporting the reader's understanding.

The following secondary sources were consulted: the Ethiopic versions of 1 Enoch, the Book of Watchers (1 Enoch 1–36), Manichaean texts published in the 1970s and 1980s, and comparative studies in ancient angelology and Jewish apocalyptic literature.

CHAPTER 5

Structure of this edition: a Unique Layout

The Book of Giants has come down to us in fragments—disordered, incomplete, and scattered across languages. For centuries, these pieces have been studied in isolation, sometimes footnoted in larger discussions of 1 Enoch or Manichaean literature, often overlooked entirely. This edition aims to bring clarity to that scattered legacy by offering not just a presentation of the text, but a way to engage with it directly and reflectively.

The core of this edition is built on a simple yet meaningful format: each fragment of the ancient text is paired with a clear, thoughtful paraphrase. The original appears on the left page, while the paraphrase appears on the right. This design allows readers to experience the raw voice of the text and, alongside it, a faithful interpretation that preserves meaning while enhancing comprehension. The decision to pair original and paraphrase was not merely stylistic. The language of ancient texts—especially apocalyptic writings like this one—is dense, symbolic, and often unfamiliar. References may be obscure, and poetic constructions can cloud meaning even for experienced readers. Rather than flattening the mystery of the text with academic footnotes or commentary, the paraphrase offers a way to move through the story with clarity while preserving the tone, depth, and theological weight of the original.

Each paraphrased passage is crafted with care, avoiding simplification or embellishment. Where the text is ambiguous, the paraphrase respects that ambiguity. Where it is symbolic, the paraphrase reflects that symbolism without forcing interpretation. The goal is not to explain the text, but to echo it in language that speaks more clearly to a modern reader, while remaining faithful to its spirit. In addition to the main body of the work, the book is framed by two key elements. The first is the extended introduction—an exploration of context, mythology, language, and meaning. This introduction offers historical background and thematic insights to prepare the reader for the deeper experience of the text itself. It does not seek to interpret or control the reading, but to open paths of understanding.

The second framing element is the appendix, focused on the figure of Enoch. More than a narrator or messenger, Enoch is the spiritual axis around which the entire story turns. His presence bridges the realms of heaven and earth, judgment and mercy. The appendix explores this role, not just within the Book of Giants, but across the broader landscape of apocalyptic and mystical literature.

In a sense, the very structure of this edition is itself symbolic. By placing ancient text and modern paraphrase side by side, we are mirroring the dual nature of the story—setting the "heavenly" original and the "earthly" explanation in dialogue. Much as Enoch stands between the divine and human realms, translating the will of Heaven into words men can grasp, the parallel columns allow the reader to stand between eras, between languages, comprehending both. This layout echoes an age-old practice: early scribes and scholars would often write a sacred verse and pen a gloss or Targum beside it, line for line. Here too, the reader is invited to move between what was revealed and what is understood. The white space between the columns becomes a contemplative pause, a silence on the page akin to the hush after a prophet speaks. In that silence, one might sense the gravity of the original words and the gentle guidance of their interpretation. In this way, form and content unite—each fragment and paraphrase becomes a little dialogue between past and present, urging the reader to linger, reflect, and listen for the echoes that connect them.

This structure—ancient text and modern paraphrase, framed by historical depth and theological reflection—is designed to offer a layered experience. It honors the mystery of the original, while guiding the reader into its heart without presumption or distortion. The story remains what it has always been: strange, powerful, and unfinished. This edition does not claim to complete it. It simply invites it to be heard again, in a voice both old and new.

CHAPTER 6

Enoch, the scribe of heaven

Among the many figures who appear in the ancient texts of the Second Temple period, none stands quite like Enoch. He is not a king, nor a prophet in the traditional sense. He does not lead armies, build altars, or perform signs before crowds. Instead, he listens. He writes. He is taken. And then, he returns—not to live among men, but to deliver messages from another realm.

In the Book of Giants, Enoch plays a singular role. The giants, desperate to understand their fate, seek him out. They know that he is no ordinary man. Though born of earth, Enoch has crossed into the realm of the holy. He has walked among the Watchers. He has stood before the Glory. He knows what is to come.

This figure did not appear suddenly in the literature. The roots of Enoch's story begin in the brief yet mysterious verses of Genesis: "Enoch walked with God; then he was no more, because God took him." No explanation is given, no elaboration offered. It is this silence that opened space for an entire tradition to grow.

By the time of the Book of Giants, Enoch had become far more than a name in a genealogy. He was the scribe of heaven, entrusted with recording divine secrets, visions of judgment, and the decrees of the Most High. In this capacity, Enoch becomes a unique presence in religious literature—a human lifted into the celestial realm not for glory, but for revelation. He is a witness, a writer, and a messenger. And in many ways, he is also a judge.

The Watchers, who once rebelled in arrogance, now turn to Enoch in fear. They ask him to intercede with heaven on their behalf. But Enoch does not offer comfort. What he brings is not forgiveness, but clarity. He records the words of their judgment and delivers them without hesitation. His authority is not his own. It is given. He does not invent visions—he is their vessel.

This function—scribe, mediator, revealer—makes Enoch a bridge between divine and human. In a world where the separation between heaven and earth is strictly guarded, Enoch is allowed to cross. But that privilege comes with a cost. He no longer belongs fully to either side. He becomes, like the text itself, a liminal being—of earth, yet beyond it.

In the Book of Giants, this in-between nature is emphasized. Enoch is approached from a distance, summoned through messengers, sought in the far reaches of heaven. He speaks, but only after traveling great distances—geographical, spiritual, and symbolic. His voice carries judgment, but also understanding. He does not mock the fallen. He does not argue. He tells them what is written.

This image of Enoch as a heavenly scribe continues in later apocalyptic texts. In 1 Enoch, he receives visions of cosmic architecture, divine calendars, angelic hierarchies, and the destiny of souls. In 2 Enoch, he ascends through the heavens and is transformed into a being of light. In 3 Enoch, he becomes Metatron, the lesser Yahweh, seated next to the Throne. But even in these exalted portrayals, the core remains: Enoch writes. He sees what others cannot. He records what must be remembered. There is something deeply human in Enoch's role. While the Watchers sought to dominate, to impose power, Enoch submits to revelation. His greatness comes not from strength, but from fidelity. He becomes the example of what it means to be entrusted with divine knowledge—to carry it, to preserve it, and to communicate it without distortion.

In a way, Enoch embodies the tension that defines the entire Book of Giants. He stands between the forces of rebellion and the silence of judgment. He does not save the giants, nor does he destroy them. He offers what heaven has decreed. No more, no less. His presence also reminds us that the sacred is not always loud. It is not always victorious. Sometimes it comes quietly, in the form of a figure who disappears from the world, only to return with visions written in stars and symbols. A figure who reminds even the mightiest that they are not beyond the reach of justice—or the possibility of remembrance.

There is a profound silence surrounding Enoch's work—an echo of the silence in heaven itself. While the earth was filled with the clamor of giants and the cries of the innocent, the heavens did not thunder in reply. No immediate bolt of lightning smote the Watchers when they fell; no angelic army descended to wage open war. Instead, the response came in a whisper carried by a single man. Heaven's answer to the cacophony of sin was a period of stillness and waiting, broken only by Enoch's solemn message. In that divine silence, judgment was already taking shape. Enoch's emergence as a messenger suggests that sometimes the absence of an immediate divine reaction is not absence at all—it is forethought. It is a quiet mourning for what must be done. Later mystics would note that God's voice often emerges from silence; here, the pattern holds true. The Watchers fill the world with violence, their sons with despair, and above them the sky is silent as stone—until Enoch speaks. The lesson hidden in that silence is awe-inspiring: the wheels of justice turn in hushed inevitability. When Enoch finally delivers Heaven's verdict, it arrives without fanfare, as simple truth. The stillness that preceded it made the words all the more devastating.

The giants sought Enoch because they knew he had seen what they could not. They feared the visions that visited them at night—the dreams of roots pulled from the ground, of scrolls cast into the sea, of trees drowned in floodwaters. They did not understand them. But Enoch did. And his words confirmed their deepest fear: that their end had been written before they even asked the question.

In the broader tradition, Enoch becomes the paradigm of divine transmission: the one who hears and writes. His name, meaning "dedicated" or "initiated," speaks to this role. He is the one drawn into mysteries—not to keep them, but to pass them on. And what he passes on is not only judgment, but insight into the structure of the universe, the order of the heavens, and the moral weight of choice.

In many ways, the story of the giants cannot be told without Enoch. They are the embodiment of transgression, but he is the witness of its consequence. Their story is violent, chaotic, and tragic. His is still, clear, and uncompromising. Where they overwhelm the earth with their presence, he disappears into the divine.

And yet, through his writing, he remains.

COMPARATIVE OVERVIEW: THE BOOK OF GIANTS VS. 1 ENOCH

Though both the Book of Giants and the Book of Watchers trace their origins to the broader Enochic tradition, they represent different ways of interpreting the same myth: the descent of the Watchers, the birth of the giants, and the divine response to their corruption. Where 1 Enoch presents a structured prophetic narrative preserved in the form of divine revelation, The Book of Giants is more fragmentary, symbol-laden, and introspective—focused less on heaven's pronouncement and more on the inner despair of the fallen. This comparative reading explores three key areas where the two texts reflect, diverge, and enrich one another.

Theme	The Book of Giants	1 Enoch (Book of Watchers)
Origin of the Giants	Born from the Watchers and human women	Same origin, with more emphasis on corruption
Narrative Structure	Fragmentary, rich in symbolic dreams	Cohesive, with structured prophetic visions
Role of Enoch	Intermediary and scribe, messenger of judgment	Prophet and heavenly guide
Dreams and Visions	Central to the text's symbolism	Visionary and cosmological descriptions
Divine Judgment	Implicit, foretold through giant's dreams	Explicit and detailed
Silence of Heaven	Recurring theme of unanswered appeals	God speaks directly through Enoch

1. Origin of the Giants

Both the Book of Watchers and the Book of Giants trace the origin of the giants to the same transgressive union: the Watchers, divine beings, descend to earth and cohabit with human women. This act crosses a sacred boundary between heaven and earth, and the resulting offspring—giants—embody the consequences of that rebellion. While 1 Enoch presents this origin with an emphasis on the corruption introduced by the Watchers, framing their act as a fundamental distortion of creation, The Book of Giants focuses more on the direct legacy of these unions: the giants themselves. The narrative picks up with their existence already assumed, and explores their thoughts, dreams, and fears from within.

In both texts, the giants are not merely physical anomalies but symbols of imbalance—creatures born of a fracture in divine order. Their very existence is a problem that demands resolution. However, the Book of Giants gives us rare access to their internal state: it allows the giants to speak, dream, and reflect, casting them not simply as monsters, but as tragic consequences of a cosmic violation.

2. Narrative Structure

The Book of Watchers unfolds in a structured, almost liturgical manner. Enoch is called by God, ascends to the heavens, witnesses divine mysteries, and delivers messages of judgment and explanation. The structure is linear and cohesive:

rebellion → revelation → punishment. The reader is guided step-by-step through a prophetic vision, with each element explained through Enoch's guided journey.

In contrast, the Book of Giants is fragmentary, dreamlike, and emotionally disjointed. The narrative does not flow from beginning to end but instead emerges in glimpses—fragments of dialogue, dream reports, and appeals for meaning. Rather than receiving direct revelation, the characters struggle to understand their own visions. This disjointedness is not a flaw but a feature: it reflects the chaos the giants inhabit. Their world is not orderly; their fate is not fully explained; their fears remain unresolved.

This difference in structure points to a deeper theological distinction. 1 Enoch is a book of revelation—clarity descending from above. The Book of Giants, by contrast, is a book of uncertainty—voices rising from below, desperate for an answer that never quite arrives.

3. Role of Enoch

In both The Book of Giants and 1 Enoch, Enoch stands at a threshold between worlds—but the way that threshold is navigated differs significantly. In 1 Enoch, his movement is vertical: he ascends into heaven, is initiated into cosmic secrets, and speaks with authority granted from above. His transformation is marked by exposure to celestial knowledge, and his voice carries the unmistakable tone of one who has seen the divine face-to-face.

CHAPTER 6

In The Book of Giants, Enoch's role is more horizontal. He is not elevated above the events, but inserted into them. The giants send emissaries to seek him; they plead with him not for prophecy, but for interpretation. He is not summoned by God, but sought out by those in distress. This makes Enoch not only a messenger but a mediator—a figure whose authority emerges not from position, but from insight.

Interestingly, his authority is never self-declared. He does not thunder with judgment; he writes. His wisdom is entrusted to tablets, not sermons. In a world flooded with chaotic dreams and fragmented voices, Enoch's role is not to command, but to clarify. He does not end the confusion, but brings a stillness in which meaning might emerge.

4. Dreams and Visions

Dreams in The Book of Giants are not decorative—they are the primary vehicle of meaning. They replace speech, interrupt action, and frame the inner lives of beings otherwise condemned to mythic stature. Through dreams, the giants experience fear, confusion, and—occasionally—truth. These are not dreams interpreted by God or angels, but by those who fear what they see. The symbolic world becomes the only world they can access.

In contrast, 1 Enoch treats visions as structured encounters with revelation. They come with context, interpreters, and a divine intention behind them. When Enoch dreams or sees, his experiences are embedded in a framework of trust: the reader knows that the visions are accurate, purposeful, and divinely sanctioned.

But in The Book of Giants, dreams come uninvited, full of terrifying symbols—trees drowning, names vanishing, fire consuming life. The giants do not know what they mean, and neither do we. The power of these dreams lies in their ambiguity. They are not messages, but omens. Their repetition is not instructional, but oppressive. They do not resolve; they intensify.

This marks a fundamental shift: 1 Enoch speaks from certainty into chaos. The Book of Giants speaks from chaos, searching for meaning. Its dreams are not there to be solved like puzzles, but to immerse the reader in the psychological torment of beings who sense their doom but cannot decipher its terms.

5. Divine Judgment

In 1 Enoch, divine judgment is a structured and vocal process. The fallen angels are named, accused, and sentenced. The judgment is not merely a theological claim—it is dramatized. Heavenly beings carry it out. The narrative reinforces the inevitability of divine order being restored through deliberate, visible action. Judgment is a moment of cosmic correction, and its authority is derived from God's direct decree.

In The Book of Giants, judgment feels less like a sentence and more like a shadow—an approaching reality perceived before it is ever declared. There is no formal courtroom, no divine speech echoing from the heavens. Instead, judgment is experienced as anticipation and interpretive dread. The giants are not punished outright in the text; they are terrified of what the dreams might mean. This fear itself becomes a form of judgment—a pre-verdict anxiety that robs them of peace before justice ever arrives.

This inversion is powerful: judgment in 1 Enoch is pronounced from on high; in The Book of Giants, it is inferred from below. We do not see God's hand strike—we see the giants flinch in expectation. It is a theology of consequence felt, not proclaimed.

6. Silence of Heaven

One of the most haunting features of The Book of Giants is what it does not say. Unlike 1 Enoch, where Heaven speaks often—through angels, visions, and through Enoch himself—The Book of Giants resonates with absence. The Watchers do not receive a direct answer. The giants' pleas are not immediately answered. Enoch is contacted, yes—but even his responses are muted, written rather than spoken, carried rather than proclaimed.

This silence is not weakness. It is weight. It presses down on the narrative, creating a sacred unease. The giants are not just afraid of punishment; they are afraid of what they do not know, of what has not been said. The divine silence in the face of their transgressions becomes its own kind of verdict.

In 1 Enoch, speech restores order. In The Book of Giants, silence creates tension. The lack of response becomes more frightening than a thunderous judgment. The unanswered dreams, the unclarified symbols, the lack of divine intervention—all build a sense of existential uncertainty. In a world that has already broken divine law, the worst possibility is not that God will speak—but that He already has, and no one understood.

CHAPTER 7

Themes and Symbols: Dreams, Judgment, Rebellion

The Book of Giants is not structured like a modern narrative. It unfolds in fragments, with shifts in voice, tone, and perspective. Yet through this fractured structure emerge themes of striking clarity—universal concerns shaped by ancient cosmology. Beneath the names and visions, the core of the story speaks of rebellion against divine order, the judgment that follows, and the strange, haunting power of dreams.

Rebellion is the seed from which the entire tale grows. The Watchers, originally angels of heaven, abandon their posts and descend to earth. Their choice is not a mistake but a deliberate act. They form a pact, a solemn oath to bind themselves together in transgression. This rebellion is not simply a question of lust or curiosity. It is a challenge to the hierarchy of creation. Beings who were once guardians of the heavens choose to cross into the human world and reshape it according to their will. Their union with human women marks the breaking of a fundamental boundary. From this breach come the giants— hybrids of heaven and earth, unnatural in both form and purpose. They are not born out of love, but out of excess. Their very existence is unstable. They devour what the world offers and turn against it when it cannot feed them. Their rebellion, inherited from their fathers, becomes physical. It is expressed in violence, hunger, and destruction.

Yet the Book of Giants does not present the giants as mindless monsters. Their thoughts, fears, and especially their dreams show complexity. These dreams become central to the narrative. They arrive uninvited, speaking truths that the giants do not want to hear. One sees a stone tablet submerged in water, dissolving until only three names remain. Another sees trees torn from the ground by a great wind and cast into the deep. Others dream of fires from heaven, of heavenly beings descending in judgment.

The dreams are symbolic, yet not obscure. Even the giants seem to understand their meaning instinctively. What they see is not just personal doom, but the end of their entire race. The dreams bring a knowledge they cannot refuse and cannot bear. They are revelations, but not of hope—revelations of consequence.

In ancient literature, dreams often serve as divine messages, offering hidden insights to those who are willing—or fated—to receive them. In this context, the dreams of the giants serve as a form of mercy. Before judgment falls, they are shown what is to come. They are not destroyed without warning. Their doom is revealed to them not in law, but in image, not by decree, but through vision. This gives the story a prophetic character: the future is not imposed suddenly, but unfolds through signs for those who can read them. Judgment, then, becomes the natural outcome of rebellion and revelation. It is not cruel or arbitrary. It is the fulfillment of what was already set in motion.

The Watchers are told that they will no longer return to the heavens. They are bound, imprisoned, and condemned to witness the destruction of their sons. The giants themselves face a flood—not only of water, but of erasure. Their names, legacies, and power will vanish from the face of the earth. They will be forgotten, except as a warning.

What makes this judgment so striking is its tone. It is not emotional. There is no anger in the heavens, no chaos in the divine response. The judgment is firm, clean, and final. The lines have been crossed. The order must be restored. The Book of Giants does not dwell on punishment as revenge, but as balance. A creation warped by heavenly disobedience must be returned to stability—even at the cost of annihilation.

And yet, the story is not without sorrow. The giants, despite their corruption, are tragic. They struggle to understand their place in the world. They seek answers, send messengers, try to reach Enoch. They are not innocent, but they are also not entirely blind. Their visions disturb them. Their questions go unanswered. Their fate is sealed before they can find the language to ask for mercy.

This sense of unresolved tension permeates the story. The giants are both symbols of transgression and figures of existential dread. Their dreams are not only prophecies—they are expressions of fear and confusion, echoes of a consciousness that knows it should not exist. In their dreams, the giants see themselves for what they are: beings out of place, cut off from both heaven and earth, fated to disappear.

Behind these themes lies a deeper structure—one of cosmic order. The Book of Giants reflects a worldview in which every being, action, and boundary has a place. When these are respected, the world is in harmony. When they are broken, the result is not simply chaos, but disintegration. The giants, in this sense, are not just individuals but symbols of imbalance. Their fall is not only personal, but cosmological.

This symbolic reading extends to other elements of the narrative. The flood is not just a punishment—it is purification. The descent of fire is not only destruction—it is the reassertion of divine presence. The silence that follows the judgment is not emptiness, but restoration.

In this light, Enoch's role becomes even more significant. He does not act. He observes, records, and transmits. His position as scribe and mediator places him outside the drama, but deeply within its meaning. He represents the possibility of understanding without corruption, of vision without rebellion. His voice, quiet and precise, is the only one that endures.

The Book of Giants, for all its missing pieces, weaves a tapestry of symbols that continue to resonate. Rebellion, judgment, and dreams are not relics of ancient fear—they are mirrors. They reflect questions that are still asked: What is the cost of crossing boundaries? How does justice emerge from silence? Can visions of destruction lead to wisdom? There are no final answers. Only fragments. But within them, meaning still burns.

Thus the saga offers us a stark meditation on divine justice. The rebellion of the Watchers and the rampage of their sons set in motion an inexorable response: not vengeful wrath, but a measured setting-right of the world. In the great flood and the binding of angels, we witness justice as balance restored. The silence that falls once the giants vanish—a silence stretching from heaven to earth—is the final seal on this judgment. It is not the gloating silence of triumph, but the hollow calm after a storm. One almost senses grief mingled with necessity. In that quiet, the ancient reader could imagine the sorrow of God, who "takes no pleasure in the death of the wicked," even as He enforces the law of creation. The giants' dreams gave them a chance to see this truth, however dimly: that the universe would be cleansed, with or without their consent. Their story, then, becomes a timeless caution. Every age has its forbidden quests, its proud overreachers. And every age faces the same choice: to heed the unheeded warnings written on the wall of night, or to learn only when the waters rise. The fragments of the Book of Giants do not lecture us directly, but the fate of its characters whispers an ageless warning. When the clamor of pride and violence dies down, what remains is a profound silence—a silence filled by the memory of what happens when the created defy their Creator. In that silence, if we listen, we might discern a path back to harmony.

CHAPTER 8

Why this book still matters

Ancient texts often speak from distant places—geographically, historically, spiritually. Their symbols are foreign, their languages lost, their voices buried under centuries of silence. And yet, some of these voices find their way back. The Book of Giants is one of them. Fragmented and often forgotten, it continues to resonate because the questions it raises are still alive. Its myth is old, but its meaning has not expired.

At its core, the Book of Giants is a meditation on limits—what happens when they are crossed, ignored, or broken. The Watchers, beings of divine origin, choose to descend. Their rebellion is not one of violence, but of interference. They step out of their place in the created order, attempting to bridge heaven and earth by force. The result is not unity, but disorder. The giants that follow are the consequence of a world out of balance. What should never have been born is now the loudest presence on the earth.

The echoes of this tension are not limited to the ancient imagination. The story of power unrestrained, of knowledge misused, of boundaries erased in the name of desire or control—these are not just spiritual concerns. They are deeply human. In every age, civilizations have asked where the line is drawn. How much knowledge is too much? When does power stop being creative and become corrupting? What is lost when the natural order is pushed beyond its design?

The giants, in this context, are more than mythic creatures. They are symbols of excess. Born from a breach in the divine-human divide, they represent what happens when things grow beyond their limits—when appetite becomes hunger without end, when strength becomes domination, when knowledge becomes manipulation. They are what the ancients feared could happen to humanity when it forgets its place in the cosmos.

Yet the Book of Giants is not just a warning. It is also a record of longing. The giants are not simply destroyers. They dream. They question. They fear. Their efforts to understand what they are and where they came from reveal a kind of broken consciousness. They reach for Enoch, the one who might explain what no one else will. There is, in their confusion, a glimpse of something tragic—a longing for meaning in the face of inevitable judgment.

That longing, too, is timeless.

In a world saturated with noise and certainty, the Book of Giants offers something different: silence, fragments, questions. It does not preach. It reveals. And in that revelation, it leaves space. Space to wonder, to reflect, to wrestle with symbols rather than conclusions.

Its characters are not heroes. Its plot is not linear. Its theology is not systematic. And yet, in all of that, it feels strangely honest. The giants' story is not told to comfort—it is told to confront. To shake the reader out of complacency, to remind them that the ancient world did not shy away from mystery, from terror, from judgment. It faced these things with open eyes and gave them form in story.

This courage—to name chaos, to describe the consequences of divine rebellion, to imagine judgment not as cruelty but as restoration—is what gives the Book of Giants its lasting power. It speaks from the margins, not the center. It was not canonized, not preserved by institutions, not embroidered into liturgy. It survived only in ruins, in parchment dust and desert shadows. And yet, it endures. Perhaps that is why it matters so deeply today. Because in its brokenness, it tells the truth. Not all stories are neat. Not all questions find answers. Sometimes the most important wisdom comes not from the center, but from what was almost lost.

The Book of Giants invites no easy readings. But it offers a mirror for those who are willing to look—not just into the past, but into the hidden corners of the present. Into our fascination with power, our relationship with knowledge, our own boundaries between creation and destruction. Its ancient voices still speak, if only in fragments. And sometimes, a fragment is enough.

CHAPTER 8

The warnings etched into this myth have echoed throughout history's great narratives. Even within the Bible's canon, we find reflections of the same cautionary theme: after the Flood purged the giants, humanity soon built the Tower of Babel, grasping again at heaven. In that story, too, a boundary was crossed, and divine action scattered the proud builders before their hubris could wreak even greater ruin. The pattern holds: for every Watcher who descends, there is a Babel that ascends—one hubris of angels answered by another of men. And beyond the Bible, the Greeks told of Prometheus, a titan who stole divine fire (knowledge) to uplift mankind and was punished by unending torment. Different details, different sympathies, but the core lesson aligns with the Book of Giants: there are gifts the gods guard carefully, powers that burn those not ready to wield them. The ancients used these stories to grapple with the same dilemma we grapple with now: where is the line between divine and human, between wisdom and folly? The resonance of the Giants' tale with the Titans, the Babel-builders, and the fire-thief of Olympus shows that multiple civilizations sensed a profound truth — that when creatures, whether divine or human, violently disrupt the cosmic order, the retribution that follows is both just and tragic. And what of today? The story of the giants feels more relevant than ever. We live in an age of immense appetites and unprecedented abilities. As a species, we have become giants of a sort—tinkering with the genomes of living beings, splitting atoms to unleash destructive power, building machines that think. We have begun to step across boundaries that our ancestors once thought immutable. The question the Book of Giants presses upon us is uncomfortably familiar: how much is too much? When does humanity's reach exceed its grasp? The tale of the Watchers and their offspring suggests that there is a moral architecture to the universe, a point at which unchecked ambition topples into catastrophe. The giants' legend reminds us that knowledge devoid of humility can consume the world that nourishes us. As we push ever closer to our own modern "forbidden arts," this ancient story's significance only sharpens. It urges caution without stifling curiosity, warning that wisdom must temper power, and reverence must guide discovery. The Book of Giants matters because it is, ultimately, a plea for balance—delivered from the dawn of civilization to the present day, from a fragment of a scroll to the heart of anyone who will pause and listen.

CHAPTER 9

Invitation to the Mystery

Not all stories arrive whole. Some come to us broken, scattered, burned at the edges, whispered across time. The Book of Giants is one of these—less a finished tale, more a sacred trace. It does not unfold like a scroll, but glimmers like stars seen through a torn sky. And yet, what remains is enough.

There is a reason these fragments survived. A reason they crossed centuries, languages, and beliefs. A reason they still disturb, still fascinate, still call. They carry weight—not just the weight of myth, but of memory. A memory not entirely human, not entirely angelic, but something in between.

To read this book is to step into that space between. Between the heavens and the earth. Between what was revealed and what was forbidden. Between voices that shouted across the void and others that fell silent before the flood.

This is not a book of conclusions. It is a door. It does not ask to be understood completely. It asks to be approached—with reverence, with patience, with openness. What you hold in your hands is not a finished text, but a living witness. A record of rebellion and ruin, of messengers and monsters, of dreams that spoke louder than armies. The giants are gone. The Watchers are bound. But their story is not done.

It continues here. In mystery. In fire. In the spaces between the lines.

For those inclined to the mystical, such spaces are where truth often hides. Jewish Kabbalists have long said that the most profound secrets dwell in the white fire of the Torah—the blank spaces around the letters—just as meaning in the Book of Giants lurks in its gaps and broken phrases. What we do not have in this story is as provocative as what we do. The absence invites us to lean in, to become participants in the act of deciphering. In a way, every reader of these fragments becomes a bit like Enoch, peering beyond the veils for wisdom. The universality of this invitation is striking. The Ethiopian Christian, treasuring the Book of Enoch, finds guidance in its mysteries; the Sufi Muslim, reflecting on Idris's ascent, seeks personal elevation through hidden knowledge; the modern seeker, regardless of creed, finds in the Giants' tale an encouragement to embrace the unknown with humility. Thus the Book of Giants does more than preserve a myth—it extends a hand across the ages, urging each of us into the silent, starry gap between understanding and wonder.

ADDITIONAL DIGITAL CONTENT

Scan the QR CODE NOW
to access all digital content!!!

+ EBOOK VERSION

3 EXTRA FANTASTIC RESOURCE
UNLOCK APOCRYPHIA'S SECRET

CHAPTER 10

THE BOOK OF GIANTS

RECONSTRUCTED FRAGMENTS AND PARAPHRASE

The following part presents the reconstructed fragments of the *Book of Giants*, based on publicly available texts and scholarly sources. Each passage is displayed in two columns: the **left column** contains the original fragment, while the **right column** provides a faithful paraphrase. Though many lines remain incomplete or damaged, the voices preserved in these texts still carry power and clarity. The paraphrase does not replace the original, but seeks to reflect its tone and meaning—illuminating the content without altering its depth.

Gaps in the text are marked. Where ambiguity exists, it is respected. The purpose is not to solve the mystery, but to listen to it with more understanding.

Let the fragments speak.

Parallel Text – Fragments and Interpretive Paraphrase

Words added for clarity appear in italic brackets and include question marks when uncertain.

The fragments are numbered for reference, though not always in a continuous or chronological sequence.

1Q23 – Fragments 9 + 14 + 15

[. . .] they knew the secrets of [. . .]
[. . .] sin was great in the Earth [. . .]
[. . .] and they killed many [. . .]
[. . .] they begat giants [. . .]

4Q531 – Fragment 3

[. . . everything that the] earth produced
[. . . the great fish . . .]
[. . .] the sky with all that grew [. . .]
[. . . fruit of] the earth and all kinds of grain and all the trees [. . .]
[. . .] beasts and reptiles . . . all creeping things of the earth and they observed all [. . .]
[. . . eve]ry harsh deed and [. . .] utterance [. . .]
[. . .] male and female, and among humans [. . .]

They descended from above, bearing with them secrets never meant for the earth.

Their wisdom, once holy, was twisted through their defiance.

As they walked among humankind, sin spread like fire—great was its weight upon the earth.

Blood was spilled in silence; many fell by their hands.

From their union with the daughters of men, giants were born—mighty, ravenous, unbound.

The angels saw the earth's richness and took it for themselves.

They consumed its harvest: the fruits, the grains, and all that grew beneath the sky.

Evenw the great beasts of the waters were not spared.

The trees bent under their hunger, and the creatures of the ground were disturbed.

They observed the order of creation—not with reverence, but with hunger.

And what they learned, they exploited.

All things that crawled, flew, or bloomed—they used them for their own desire.

They committed every violent deed, and spoke words of blasphemy and power.

Even among humans, they sowed division between male and female, twisting the bonds of life.

What was once called good, they defiled.

What was once in harmony, they shattered.

1Q23 FRAGMENT 1 + 6

[. . . two hundred]
donkeys, two hundred asses, two hundred . . . rams of the]
flock, two hundred goats, two hundred [. . . beast of the]
field from every animal, from every [bird . . .]
[. . .] for miscegenation [. . .]

4Q531 FRAGMENT 2

[. . .] they defiled [. . .]
[. . . they begot] giants and monsters [. . .]
[. . .] they begot, and, behold, all [the earth was corrupted . . .]
[. . .] with its blood and by the hand of [. . .]
[giant's] which did not suffice for them and [. . .]
[. . .] and they were seeking to devour many [. . .]
[. . .]
[. . .] the monsters attacked it.

Two hundred of the Watchers turned their gaze from heaven to the creatures of the earth.

Not only mankind drew their desire—they chose beasts of the field, birds of the air, and all living things.

From donkeys to goats, from rams to wild animals, they sought to corrupt the order set in creation.

They mingled their essence with flesh not meant for them.

Through this miscegenation, unnatural offspring began to multiply.

From these unions came giants and monsters—twisted forms of life, neither beast nor spirit, but something in between.

The earth, once fertile, groaned under the weight of their presence.

The very soil drank blood. Violence spread like roots under every step they took.

The giants were not satisfied. Their hunger grew beyond measure, and their cruelty matched their size.

They devoured what they could find—and when nothing was left, they turned on one another.

The corruption had no limit.

Even the monsters turned upon the world, and their rage devoured it.

Nothing was left untouched. Nothing remained clean.

4Q532 COLUMN 2 – FRAGMENTS 1–6

[...] flesh [...]

all [...] monsters [...] will be [...]

[...] they would arise [...] lacking in true knowledge [...] because [...]

[...] the earth [grew corrupt ...] mighty [...]

[...] they were considering [...]

[...] from the angels upon [...]

[...] in the end it will perish and die [...]

[...] they caused great corruption in the [earth ...] [... this did not] suffice to [...]

"they will be [...]"

2Q26

[The floodwaters?] they drenched the tablet in the wa[ter ...]

[... And?] the waters went up over the [tablet ...]

[... And then?] they lifted out the tablet from the water of [...]

The flesh of the world was no longer pure.

Monsters roamed freely—aberrant beings whose thoughts were empty, devoid of true knowledge.

Their origins were confusion; their existence a mark of defilement.

They rose in power, but not in wisdom.

And as they multiplied, the earth was further corrupted by their presence.

Might was mistaken for greatness, and destruction was mistaken for strength.

Some began to reflect.

Whispers moved among them—of things seen in dreams, of voices not their own.

The angels from whom they were born could not answer what they had set in motion.

It was said that in the end, all of it would perish.

Still, the corruption continued. What had been done was not enough—they sought more.

And in their greed, they brought ruin to the very ground beneath them.

But then came a dream.

Mahway, son of Barakel, saw a vision in the night.

A tablet was lowered into the deep waters. Waves rose over it and submerged it completely.

When the tablet was drawn back out, only three names remained.

All the rest had been washed away—erased, forgotten.

The meaning was heavy. Few would survive. The rest would drown in judgment

4Q530 FRAGMENT 7

[. . . this vision] is for cursing and sorrow.

I am the one who confessed

[. . .] the whole group of the castaways that I shall go to [. . .]

[. . . the spirits of the sl]ain complaining about their killers and crying out

[. . .] that we shall die together and be made an end of

[. . .] much and I will be sleeping, and bread

[. . .] for my dwelling; the vision and also

[. . .] entered into the gathering of the giants [. . .]

6Q8

[. . .] Ohya and he said to Mahway [. . .]

[. . .] without trembling.

Who showed you all this vision, [my] brother?

[. . .] Barakel, my father, was with me.

[. . .] Before Mahway had finished telling what [he had seen . . .]

[. . . he said] to him, Now I have heard wonders! If a barren woman gives birth [. . .]

"This vision," said Mahway, "is filled with sorrow and curse. I alone have spoken of it openly."

Among the sons of the fallen, he stood apart. He told them of what he saw, of those left behind, of the slain whose spirits cried out for justice—murdered, yet not silent.

Their voices rose from the ground, demanding answers, naming their killers.

Mahway saw the truth: "We too shall perish. All of us. We will fall together, and be no more."

He spoke of the weariness he felt. Of sleep overtaking him. Of the hunger that would not leave. He entered the council of the giants, the gathering place of the mighty.

There, the vision still clung to him.

Ohya turned to him. His voice was steady, but the question was heavy.

"Who showed you this vision, brother?" Mahway answered, "My father, Barakel, was with me."

Before the vision was even fully told, Ohya interrupted: "These are wonders I have never heard. If even a barren woman gives birth, then what will become of us?"

4Q530 FRAGMENT 4

[There]upon Ohya said to Ha[hya . . .]

[. . . to be destroyed] from upon the earth and [. . .]

[. . . the ea]rth.

When

[. . .] they wept before [the giants . . .]

4Q530 FRAGMENT 7

[. . .] your strength [. . .]

[. . .]

Thereupon Ohya [said] to Hahya [. . .]

Then he answered, It is not for us but for Azaiel, for he did [. . . the children of] angels

are the giants, and they would not let all their loved ones] be neglected

[. . . we have] not been cast down; you have strength [. . .]

Hahyah listened in silence. Then Ohya said to him: "It has been decreed that we will be erased from the earth.

The ground beneath us, which once gave life, will turn against us."

And when the others heard these words, they wept.

The mighty ones, the giants of renown, shed tears before one another.

Ohya turned to Hahyah and spoke again.

"This burden we carry," he said, "it is no longer ours to lift.

The fault lies with Azaiel—he is the one who led us here."

The children of the angels, born through forbidden union, had become giants. And now, those same giants sought to protect the ones they loved from the consequences that followed.

"But we," Ohya said, "have not yet fallen.

We still hold strength… even if the heavens have turned against us."

THE BOOK OF GIANTS

CHAPTER 10

4Q531 FRAGMENT 1

[. . . I am a] giant, and by the mighty strength of my arm and my own great strength

[. . . any]one mortal, and I have made war against them;

but I am not

[. . .] able to stand against them, for my opponents

[. . .] reside in [Heav]en, and they dwell in the holy places.

And not

[. . . they] are stronger than I.

[. . .] of the wild beast has come, and the wild man they call [me].

[. . .] Then Ohya said to him, I have been forced to have a dream

[. . .] the sleep of my eyes [vanished], to let me see a vision. Now I know that on [. . .]

[. . .]

[. . .] Gilgamesh [. . .]

Then another voice rose—one of might and memory.

"I am a giant," said the warrior. "By the strength of my arm, I have overcome mortal men. I have fought and crushed many. But now I cannot stand."

His voice trembled. "For those who oppose me... they do not walk the earth. They dwell in the heavens, in the holy places above."

His strength, once unmatched, was now powerless against the forces of the divine. "They are stronger than I."

They had called him wild beast, and wild man—Gilgamesh. But even he, the fiercest of them all, could no longer deny what had come.

Then Ohya spoke again: "A vision was forced upon me in my sleep. It took away my rest and opened my eyes. Now I see what awaits."

He paused. "It is no longer hidden."

CHAPTER 10

6Q8 FRAGMENT 2

three of its roots [. . .]
[while] I was [watching,] there came
[. . . they moved the roots into]
this garden, all of them, and
not [. . .]

4Q530 COLUMN 2

[. . . The vision ?]
concerns the death of our souls [. . .
[and of ( ) ?] and all his comrades,
[and Oh]ya told them what
Gilgamesh said to him
[. . .] and it was said [. . .]
"concerning [. . .] the leader has
cursed the potentates"
[. . . the king has cursed the princes]
and the giants were glad at his words.
Then he turned and left [. . .]

Ohya saw another vision. A tree stood before him—its branches stripped, its trunk fallen. Only three of its roots remained.

He watched as they were lifted, taken from the earth and moved elsewhere, into a garden not of this world. All the rest was left behind. Uprooted. Forgotten.

This dream struck deeply, echoing Mahway's vision of the tablet submerged.

But Ohya, unwilling to accept the truth, searched for another meaning. He claimed the dream was not for them—not for the giants.

"It concerns Azazel," he said, "and those who follow him."

Later, he spoke again: "This vision speaks of the death of our souls. Of Azazel and his companions—perhaps them, not us."

He repeated what Gilgamesh had told him. And then someone spoke—maybe a messenger, maybe a voice within the dream—saying: "The ruler has cursed the kings. The leader has condemned the princes."

The giants, hearing this, rejoiced. They believed the curse was not on them, but on the great ones of the earth—those who held power in the world of men.

Encouraged by this thought, Ohya turned and walked away. But peace did not follow.

New dreams came to them. Not just to the giants, but even to the monsters—the twisted offspring of twisted unions. Visions returned, dark and persistent.

Their meaning was unclear, but their message was certain: The end was drawing near.

CHAPTER 10

UNNAMED FRAGMENT

*Thereupon two of them had dreams
and the sleep of their eye fled from them,
and they arose and came to [. . .]
[. . . and told them?] their dreams,
and said in the assembly of [their comrades] the monsters
[. . . In] my dream I was watching this very night
[and there was a garden . . . of trees with?] gardeners and they were watering
[. . . two hundred trees,
and] large shoots came out of their root [and they drank?]
[. . .] all the water, and the [a?] fire burned all
[the garden . . .]
They found the giants to tell them
[the dream . . .]*

Then two among them were struck by visions.

Sleep fled from their eyes, and they rose in the night, restless. They sought the others—monsters like themselves—and gathered in council.

There, before all, they spoke of what they had seen.

"This very night," said one, "I watched in a dream. A garden lay before me, vast and green. There were trees beyond number, and gardeners moved among them, tending the roots. They watered the trees with care—there were two hundred of them, tall and proud. From their roots sprang thick shoots, and they drank deeply from the earth."

"But then, the water was no more. It vanished.

And fire came. It burned through the garden, consuming all. The trees, the soil, the life that once was—turned to ash."

The dreamers, disturbed by what they had seen, went to find the giants.

They brought the vision before them, heavy with fear.

No one spoke of interpretation.

The meaning was already clear.

CHAPTER 10

[... to Enoch] the noted scribe, and he will interpret for us

the dream.

Thereupon his fellow Ohya declared and said to the giants,

I too had a dream this night, O giants,

and, behold, the Ruler of Heaven came down to earth

[...]

and such is the end of the dream.

[Thereupon] all the giants [and monsters] grew afraid

and called Mahway.

He came to them and the giants pleaded with him and sent him to Enoch

[the noted scribe].

They said to him,

Go [...] to you that

[...] you have heard his voice.

And he said to him,

He will [... and] interpret the dreams [...]

And they said among themselves, "We must go to Enoch, the renowned scribe.

He will understand. He will interpret these dreams for us."

Then Ohya stood before the others and spoke: "I too have dreamed, O giants. And in my vision, I saw the Ruler of Heaven descend to earth. He came down from on high…"

His words trailed off. That was all he could say. But the message was clear.

Fear seized them all—the giants and the monsters alike. They called for Mahway, son of Barakel, and when he came, they pleaded with him. They begged him to go.

"Find Enoch, the scribe," they said. "You have heard his voice before. You know his path. Go to him. Ask what these dreams mean. Ask what is to come."

And Mahway agreed. He would journey beyond the edges of the world.

He would cross the veil, and seek the one who speaks for heaven.

4Q530 COLUMN 3

[. . .] how long the giants have to live. [. . .]

[. . . he mounted up in the air]

like strong winds, and flew with his hands like ea[gles . . . he left behind]

the inhabited world and passed over Desolation, the great desert [. . .]

and Enoch saw him and hailed him,

and Mahway said to him [. . . A dream has been sent?]

hither and thither a second time to Mahway

[. . . The giants await

your words, and all the monsters of the earth. If [. . .] has been carried [. . .]

from the days of [. . .] their [. . .]

and they will be added [. . .]

[. . .] we would know from you their meaning [. . .]

[. . . two hundred tr]ees that from heaven [came down . . .]

4Q530 FRAGMENT 2

The scribe [Enoch . . .] [. . .]

"How long shall we live?" That was the unspoken question that haunted them. Mahway rose through the skies like a wind unbound.

With outstretched hands like eagles' wings, he soared above the earth. He left behind all that was known and crossed the Great Desolation—the wilderness beyond life, the borders of the forgotten world. There, in a place untouched by man, he found Enoch. The scribe saw him and greeted him.

And Mahway spoke: "A second time I have come. A dream has been sent again. The giants await your answer. The monsters too.

We do not understand what we have seen. Symbols, visions… two hundred trees descending from heaven…" He paused.

"If these dreams were written long ago, if their meaning has been sealed since the beginning, let us now know the truth."

Enoch listened. And then, the scribe wrote. He did not speak aloud. He inscribed his message upon a tablet—a silent decree to be carried back across the desert, across the skies, back to those who feared what they already knew.

The message was clear. Their time was over. Yet in the silence between the lines, perhaps there was still a space—not for escape, but for understanding. Not for survival, but for repentance.And thus, Enoch's voice, once again, became the voice of heaven.

Closing Note – End of the Record

With Enoch's final message, the account comes to an end.

The giants, once proud and powerful, are left waiting—not for answers, but for consequences they can no longer escape.

Their dreams have been shared.

Their fears have taken shape.

And in seeking Enoch, they faced the truth they already suspected.

No redemption is offered, no alternative path given.

Only a clear response, written by the one chosen to carry the voice of judgment.

The record is now complete.

What follows is no longer part of their story, but part of what has been written from the beginning.

APPENDIX 1
ENOCH, THE CELESTIAL MEDIATOR

Between Worlds: The Role of the Celestial Scribe

Enoch stands at the threshold of two realms. Unlike the giants—born of heaven and earth in defiance—Enoch crosses the boundary not through rebellion, but by invitation. He is taken, not fallen. Chosen, not self-exalted. In the ancient imagination, this places him in a category unlike any other figure. He belongs to earth by birth, but not by fate. He becomes the bridge between the divine and the human, walking the space few are permitted to enter.

His most essential function is that of a scribe. In a world where memory is sacred and the spoken word holds power, the one who writes is more than an observer—he is a vessel of permanence. Enoch records what is seen in visions, what is spoken by angels, and what is decreed from on high. He does not merely receive knowledge; he preserves it for those who cannot ascend. His writing becomes testimony.

This role is not passive. To write divine decrees is to carry authority. Not the authority of command, but of witness. Enoch bears witness to judgment before it falls, to rebellion before it spreads, to mercy even when it is veiled. His neutrality makes him powerful. He does not act out of vengeance or desire. He listens, watches, and transmits.

In the Book of Giants, this is why he is sought. The Watchers and their offspring turn to him not because he has power to change their fate, but because they recognize he speaks truth that is not his own. He is the only one they trust to carry their pleas, their dreams, their questions. They know that he stands where none of them can. He has entered the mystery—and returned.

The reverence for Enoch's scribal role is echoed across diverse traditions. In the *Book of Jubilees* (an ancient retelling of Genesis), Enoch is described as the first man ever to learn writing and knowledge, a holy man who diligently wrote down the judgment of the world and all the deeds of the Watchers. By that account, he became the original recorder of sin and righteousness—a precursor to all later scripture. Likewise, in Islamic tradition, Enoch is identified with the prophet *Idris*, whom the Quran extols as "truthful" and whom later commentators celebrate as the first to write with a pen. In Muslim lore, Idris/Enoch is credited with introducing writing, astronomy, and other sciences to mankind under God's guidance. These parallels in Jewish and Islamic sources underscore a singular point: Enoch was seen not merely as a character in a story, but as the *initiator of wisdom* for humanity. Whether inscribing heavenly secrets on tablets or teaching early humans to record knowledge, he stands as the patron of scribes and scholars. Across cultures, Enoch's pen becomes as mighty as any sword of flame—his writings a bridge carrying divine truth down to earth.

The Heavenly Ascent: Enoch's Transformation

The moment Enoch is taken from the earth marks a shift not only in his story, but in the spiritual landscape of ancient literature. He is not taken in death, nor claimed in battle. He is drawn upward—alive, aware, and chosen. The heavens receive him, and there, he is changed.

Unlike other figures who encounter the divine briefly—such as Moses on Sinai or Elijah in his chariot—Enoch does not return unchanged or untouched. His ascent is not temporary. He becomes part of the celestial realm. In later traditions, this transformation is described in detail: his flesh is turned to flame, his eyes become fire, his voice becomes like the sound of many waters. He is clothed in glory, set among the angels, and given a name known only in the higher spheres.

Yet even in the earliest versions of his story, this elevation is more than symbolic. It establishes him as a witness who has seen both sides. He is not like Elijah, taken and hidden. Nor like Moses, who glimpsed the divine from the cleft of a rock. Enoch moves freely through the heavens, guided by angelic hosts, shown the architecture of creation, and entrusted with visions of time itself.

This transformation sets him apart. He is not simply a prophet, but a prototype—a figure of what humanity can be when called to serve not power, but truth. His change is not self-willed. It is granted. And in receiving it, he becomes a mediator—not because he pleads, but because he knows.

To ascend is to see. To be transformed is to carry what was seen back into a world that has forgotten how to listen.

Other traditions echo and celebrate this extraordinary fate of Enoch. In the Quran, it is written of Idris (Enoch): "We raised him to a high station" — a simple statement that Muslim interpreters have understood to mean that Enoch was taken alive into heaven by God's mercy. Islamic folklore embellishes this, describing how Idris journeyed through the spheres of the heavens, much like Enoch's own heavenly travelogue. In the Ethiopian Orthodox Church, Enoch's ascension is accepted as fact, and he is revered as a saint who dwells in the presence of God to this day. Ethiopian hymns and liturgies sometimes name Enoch alongside Elijah as holy ones assumed into heaven. Such acknowledgments in two major world faiths reinforce the marvel of Enoch's transformation. To Muslims, he stands as a virtuous prophet uniquely honored by God; to Ethiopian Christians, he is a living testament to divine favor. The idea that a just man might be taken bodily into paradise struck these communities not as fantasy, but as a promise: a sign that closeness to the Creator can transcend even death. Enoch's ascent, therefore, is more than one man's miracle—it is a beacon of hope that echoes through Judaism, Christianity, and Islam alike, pointing to the possibility of unity between mortal and divine.

A Voice of Judgment: Enoch and the Watchers

When the Watchers realized the consequences of their descent, it was not to heaven they turned—it was to Enoch. Though once mighty and radiant, these beings who had broken divine law found themselves unable to speak directly to the Creator. Cut off, they sought out the one who could still walk between realms. They pleaded through their dreams, through their sons, through messengers. Enoch was their last hope.

But Enoch did not argue on their behalf. He did not bargain or intercede in the way a priest might. Instead, he brought a message—stern, unwavering, already written. He became the voice of judgment, not because he passed it, but because he was entrusted to carry it. He did not soften its edges. He did not reinterpret its meaning. He simply delivered what was decreed.

This neutrality gives Enoch a unique moral authority. He is not emotionally entangled. He is not moved by fear or pity. He remains steady, focused, precise. The Watchers had crossed a line that could not be uncrossed. Their offspring had filled the earth with violence. The balance had been broken, and the sentence was clear.

Enoch's voice, in this context, is not cold—but solemn. It carries the weight of heaven's silence and the certainty of irreversible truth. His words are not threats, but revelations of what already is. Judgment, once spoken through him, is no longer a future possibility—it is an approaching certainty. And when he speaks,

the Watchers do not protest. They mourn. Because in his voice, they hear the final echo of a justice they once abandoned.

In early Christian apocalyptic lore, there arose a belief that Enoch's role as the herald of judgment was not finished—that he would return in the last days of the world. Some church traditions identified Enoch as one of the prophesied "two witnesses" in the Book of Revelation, destined to appear before the end of time to confront a wicked world. In this view, Enoch, paired with Elijah (another prophet who ascended without dying), will again walk the earth, preaching repentance and pronouncing judgment against a new generation of giants in spirit—the tyrants and deceivers of the end times. It is a striking extension of his biblical role: Enoch's ancient confrontation with the Watchers becomes a template for a future mission. Though this teaching was never universally adopted, it persisted in Christian legend. It underscores how enduring Enoch's image as the uncompromising truth-teller is. Millennia after he delivered the Watchers' sentence, believers could still imagine Enoch standing once more in a corrupted world, fearless and ageless, speaking the final warning from God. Whether one takes this literally or symbolically, the message is consistent: the voice that pronounced judgment before the Flood may yet be heard again when humanity reaches its ultimate crisis.

APPENDIX 1

Enoch and Divine Knowledge: Secrets and Silence

Among all the roles attributed to Enoch, one of the most profound is that of a keeper of secrets. He is not just a messenger, but a custodian of the mysteries. In apocalyptic literature, he is shown recording the courses of the stars, the phases of the moon, the names and ranks of angels, and the calendar of divine time. This knowledge is not ornamental—it defines the structure of reality.

Unlike the Watchers, who shared forbidden teachings with humanity—magic, weaponry, enchantments—Enoch receives his knowledge lawfully. He is shown, not because he demanded to see, but because he was chosen. He watches the movements of the heavens, walks among cosmic halls, and listens as angels explain the order of creation. He writes it all down—not for power, but for remembrance.

This contrast is critical. The Watchers gave knowledge that distorted. They offered secrets prematurely, without permission, driven by desire. What they gave led to imbalance and destruction. Enoch, by contrast, receives knowledge in silence and obedience. He does not use it to manipulate. He does not teach it to gain followers. He records it, protects it, and waits until the time is right to reveal what he has seen.

Even his silence is meaningful. In some texts, Enoch is shown withholding certain truths. There are things too sacred, too dangerous, to speak plainly. In this, he becomes not only a witness to mystery, but a guardian of it.

Through Enoch, divine knowledge is restored to its rightful place—not as a weapon, but as a trust. He teaches that revelation is not about control. It is about timing, responsibility, and reverence.

Over the centuries, storytellers and scholars wove legends to illustrate Enoch's careful stewardship of divine wisdom. One Hebrew tradition claims that Enoch, foreseeing the Flood, inscribed the sum of heavenly knowledge onto pillars of stone and brick, so that the survivors of catastrophe would not be deprived of truth. Though the waters might wipe away cities, the secrets of creation and the fate of the Watchers would endure, carved in an indestructible record. This legend, whether taken literally or symbolically, portrays Enoch as a preserver of knowledge for the future, anticipating and outsmarting oblivion. Likewise, the later sages of Jewish mysticism (the Kabbalists) often cited Enoch as an exemplar of *sod* — the hidden, the secret. They taught that profound truths (like the workings of angels or the emanations of God's presence) should be concealed from the unready, revealed only to the pure of heart. So too, Enoch's story is one of restraint: he unveils what is lawful and seals up what would harm. The Watchers shattered heavenly silence with public secrets, but Enoch keeps holy silence when needed. His lore became a cornerstone for the principle that *not all knowledge is fit for all ears*. In a sense, Enoch is the patron saint of sacred secrecy. He reminds us that *how* and *when* wisdom is shared can determine whether it heals or destroys. His gentle withholding of certain mysteries is as important as the revelations he delivers—teaching us that sometimes reverence is expressed by *silence*, by bearing truth in one's heart until the world is ready to receive it.

From Man to Metatron: The Evolution of Enoch in Later Traditions

The story of Enoch does not end with the Book of Giants, nor with his appearances in early apocalyptic writings. Over time, his figure continues to evolve, expanding beyond his role as scribe and prophet. In later Jewish mystical literature, Enoch is transformed—not metaphorically, but cosmically—into Metatron, the highest of angels, the celestial vice-regent often called the "lesser Yahweh."

This development appears most fully in 3 Enoch, a mystical Hebrew text from the early medieval period. There, Enoch is taken into heaven and, through a process of divine exaltation, is renamed Metatron. He is given robes of glory, a throne beside the Throne, and seventy names. His stature reaches such heights that even the angels tremble before him. His voice becomes thunder, and his presence nearly indistinguishable from that of the Most High.

This transformation is staggering—but it does not come without tension. Metatron remains a created being, and though clothed in splendor, he is not God. In fact, some texts record a divine rebuke when Metatron is mistakenly worshipped. His exaltation is real, but it remains bound by divine limits. He is powerful, but not autonomous. He reflects glory; he does not originate it.

The evolution from Enoch to Metatron reflects both continuity and departure. The continuity lies in the central theme: a human who becomes more than human through proximity to the divine. In 1 Enoch and 2 Enoch, the transformation is gradual. Enoch is shown visions, taken into higher realms, and sometimes clothed in light. But he retains his humility, his role as a recorder and observer. In 3 Enoch, that role expands into one of cosmic authority.

The departure, however, is theological. Early apocalyptic texts emphasize Enoch's humility and function. Later mystical writings elevate him to a position of near-divine mediation. He becomes a figure through whom prayers are passed, decrees are issued, and the heavenly court is managed. He no longer only sees the divine order—he helps maintain it.

In this way, Enoch becomes not only a bridge between heaven and earth, but between eras of spiritual thought. From apocalyptic warning to mystical wonder, his figure continues to speak across traditions.

Enoch's journey from mortal to Metatron is paralleled by his journey across cultures. In the highlands of Ethiopia, Enoch never faded into obscurity; instead, he was enshrined as an enduring part of scripture. The Ethiopian Orthodox Church kept the *Book of Enoch* (1 Enoch) in its biblical canon, which meant that for Ethiopian Christians, the visions of Enoch and the fall of the Watchers remained familiar teachings. To them, Enoch was not a distant myth but a revered patriarch who prophesied the Flood and gazed upon God's majesty. This preservation had profound effects: when European scholars "rediscovered" Enoch's book in the 18th century (through Ethiopian manuscripts), it was as if a lost voice had returned from antiquity, thanks to Ethiopia's faithfulness. Meanwhile, in the Islamic world, Enoch found new life as *Idris*. The Quran mentions Idris alongside the likes of Noah and Abraham, calling him "exceedingly truthful, a prophet." Muslim tradition holds that Idris did not die but was raised to heaven, much like the Enoch of Genesis. As Islamic civilization encountered Greek philosophy and Hermetic lore, some scholars fused identities and concluded that Idris was the same as Hermes Trismegistus, the legendary sage. Thus Enoch-Idris-Hermes became a composite figure symbolizing the transmission of primeval wisdom to mankind. Alchemists, astronomers, and philosophers in the Islamic Golden Age revered Idris as the originator of their arts. The fact that Enoch's persona could be woven into the fabric of Islam and even occult wisdom speaks to his universal appeal. He is at once a scriptural prophet, a mystical angel-king, and a culture hero credited with inventing sciences. Few figures have traveled so far from their origin and yet retained their essence. In all these transformations, one thread remains: Enoch represents the human aspiration to reach the divine, and the divine willingness to raise the human.

Mediator of Justice and Mercy: Enoch's Enduring Symbolism

In all his forms—prophet, scribe, witness, angel—Enoch remains a symbol of balance. His story threads the tension between judgment and mercy, silence and revelation, distance and closeness. He does not belong to the realm of destruction, but he stands in its shadow. He does not speak for the guilty, but he hears them. He does not beg for mercy, but his presence keeps the path to it open.

What sets Enoch apart is his stillness. He is not driven by wrath or pity. He listens, records, delivers. In a world of clamor—of giants devouring, of Watchers pleading, of voices crying out from a broken earth—his quiet fidelity holds the center. Through him, divine justice is made known. Not as vengeance, but as necessary restoration.

At the same time, Enoch never becomes distant or cold. His ascent does not detach him from humanity—it expands his role within it. He becomes the one who has seen what others cannot, yet still carries that knowledge with compassion. Not indulgence. Not indifference. But a kind of holy clarity. He knows that mercy is not the opposite of judgment, but its companion.

This is why Enoch endures. Not because his name appears often in sacred texts, but because of what he represents: the human who listens, the mortal who ascends, the messenger who does not distort the message. He reminds us that mystery is not always to be solved, but to be honored. That truth, when carried faithfully, needs no embellishment.

Enoch is the voice between voices—the mediator who neither condemns nor excuses, but speaks what must be spoken.

And sometimes, that is the holiest task of all.

JUDAH

BARUCH
BARUCH

TESTAMENTS OF THE TWELVE PATRIARCHS

EZEKIEL
EZEKIEL

GOSPEL OF TRUTH
ASCENSION OF ISAIAH

ENOCH

TESTAMENT OF ABRAHAM
2 BARUCH

2 ENOCH
1 ENOCH

APPENDIX 2
CONNECTIONS WITH OTHER APOCRYPHAL TEXTS

Voices Across the Texts

The Book of Giants does not stand alone. Although preserved only in fragments and long overshadowed by more complete apocryphal writings, its themes, characters, and structure reveal deep connections with a wide range of ancient texts. These parallels are not coincidental—they reflect a shared symbolic language and a common worldview rooted in early Jewish apocalyptic thought.

From the fall of the Watchers to Enoch's role as mediator, the narrative of the Book of Giants intersects meaningfully with writings such as the Book of Watchers, Jubilees, and 2 Enoch. These works, while differing in tone and emphasis, draw from the same mythological and theological foundation: a cosmos shaped by rebellion, judgment, revelation, and the boundaries between the divine and the human.

This study explores several key apocryphal texts that resonate with the Book of Giants. It is not a comprehensive comparison, but a focused examination of thematic and narrative intersections—points where ancient voices seem to echo one another across time and tradition.

Understanding these connections not only enriches the reading of the Book of Giants, but also highlights its place within a larger, interwoven tradition of hidden and visionary writings.

The Book of Watchers (1 Enoch 6–36)

Among the earliest and most influential apocalyptic writings in Jewish tradition, the Book of Watchers provides the foundational narrative for the myth of the fallen angels and their monstrous offspring. As chapters 6–36 of the composite work known as 1 Enoch, this text lays the groundwork for what later becomes central in the Book of Giants—a story of divine rebellion, hybrid beings, and cosmic judgment.

The Book of Watchers begins with a dramatic descent. Two hundred angels, led by a chief named Semjaza, look down upon the daughters of men and, moved by desire, make a pact to descend together to earth. Their decision is deliberate, not accidental. By swearing an oath of mutual commitment atop Mount Hermon, they bind themselves to the act and to one another, fully aware that they are crossing a divine boundary.

Once on earth, the Watchers take wives from among human women and beget children. These offspring are not ordinary—enormous in stature and appetite, they devour all the produce of the earth, then turn on animals, and finally on mankind. The text portrays these giants as destructive forces, physical embodiments of disorder and excess. Their very existence disrupts the balance of creation. This story, as recorded in 1 Enoch, is not merely a tale of lust or punishment. It is a myth of sacred order being torn apart. The Watchers, once celestial beings assigned to watch over humanity, violate their role by taking part in earthly affairs. Their union with humans is not only unnatural but a direct violation of the separation between heaven and earth—one of the central boundaries in biblical cosmology.

The consequences of this rebellion unfold quickly. The giants begin to devastate the earth, but the corruption is not only physical. The Watchers also impart forbidden knowledge to humanity. They teach the cutting of roots, the use of enchantments, astrology, the making of weapons, cosmetics, and other arts that, in this context, are associated with deception and self-exaltation. Humanity becomes complicit in the fall, not through its own initiative, but by receiving divine secrets prematurely and misusing them. In response, the earth itself cries out. The blood of the innocent, shed by the giants, becomes a voice that reaches heaven. The archangels—Michael, Gabriel, Raphael, and Uriel—are sent to intervene. God, in a strikingly judicial tone, commands them to bind the Watchers, destroy the giants, and purify the earth. A flood is decreed, not as a random punishment, but as a cosmic cleansing of a corrupted creation.

This sequence—descent, corruption, intercession, and judgment—forms the full arc of the Watchers narrative and directly anticipates the Book of Giants. In fact, the Book of Giants should be seen not as a separate or competing tradition, but as a continuation and elaboration of the same myth. Many of the names found in the Qumran fragments of the Book of Giants (Semjaza, Mahway, Ohya, Hahyah) trace their roots to the world first described in 1 Enoch. The difference lies in tone and focus: while the Book of Watchers centers on the fall and its consequences from a heavenly and prophetic perspective, the Book of Giants shifts attention to the psychological and existential turmoil of the giants themselves.

In the Book of Watchers, Enoch is portrayed as a righteous man chosen to act as intercessor. The Watchers appeal to him, begging him to speak to God on their behalf. He travels through the heavens, witnesses cosmic secrets, and returns with a message of final judgment. His role as intermediary is firm, but not merciful—he does not negotiate their fate; he simply delivers what has been decreed. This portrayal sets the stage for the even more central role Enoch plays in the Book of Giants, where he becomes the only figure the giants trust to explain their dreams and their destiny. The continuity between the two texts is not just thematic, but literary. Both works share narrative motifs—divine descent, unnatural offspring, dreams foretelling destruction, Enoch's mediation, and the inevitability of judgment. Both explore the tension between heavenly knowledge and earthly transgression, and both uphold the idea that creation has limits that, once crossed, demand restoration through force. What the Book of Giants adds is perspective: it gives voice to the fallen. It offers fragments of fear, confusion, and despair from within the doomed generation. But those fragments would be unintelligible without the structure established by the Book of Watchers. The two texts form a narrative dyad: one frames the fall, the other echoes its consequences.

In this way, 1 Enoch 6–36 is not only a source but a lens. It allows the Book of Giants to be read not as a strange tale from the margins, but as part of a deep and enduring apocalyptic vision—a vision that begins with angels descending and ends with a flood washing the earth clean.

The Book of Jubilees

The Book of Jubilees, often called "Little Genesis," is one of the most important apocryphal texts for understanding how early Jewish tradition sought to reframe and formalize ancient stories. Written in the second century BCE, most likely in Hebrew and later preserved in Ge'ez, the text retells the events of Genesis and parts of Exodus within a strict chronological and theological structure. This rewriting is not merely a stylistic exercise—it is a theological intervention. In doing so, Jubilees preserves and expands the story of the Watchers and the Giants, incorporating them into a sacred timeline and assigning them a specific place within divine history.

Unlike the more visionary and symbolic Book of Watchers, Jubilees is legalistic and precise. It recasts the sin of the Watchers not only as a rebellion, but as a serious violation of divine law that affects the entire order of creation. The descent of the angels is placed within a clearly dated framework: it occurs in the second week of the tenth jubilee, precisely after the flood narrative begins to take shape. The author of Jubilees does not merely describe the event—he indicts it. The sin of the Watchers is presented as a direct cause of the corruption of mankind and one of the primary justifications for the coming of the flood. In Jubilees, the union between angels and human women is condemned in the strongest terms. The offspring of this union—the giants—are described as beings who brought violence, chaos, and bloodshed to the earth. They consumed everything, just as in 1 Enoch, but here their existence also represents a defilement of the purity of creation. There is no hint of tragic ambiguity, no sense that the giants are confused or seeking redemption. Their existence is a threat that must be erased. The flood, therefore, is not simply a punishment—it is a necessary act of cosmic purification.

One of the most striking aspects of Jubilees is how it integrates the story of the Watchers and their offspring into a broader legal and moral worldview. Sin is not only personal; it is structural. The actions of the Watchers violate the order of heaven and earth, and the consequences affect all generations. The narrative does not treat this rebellion as mythological or symbolic—it is framed as a real historical event that justifies specific divine interventions and supports the idea of an unchanging moral law. Enoch also appears in Jubilees, but his role is less central than in the Book of Watchers or Book of Giants. He is still a righteous man, a scribe, and a witness to heavenly truths, but he functions more as a keeper of knowledge and calendars than a mediator between fallen angels and divine judgment. He is credited with establishing the 364-day calendar, essential to the proper observance of festivals and Sabbaths. His wisdom serves the purpose of religious order rather than mystical revelation. Still, his presence confirms the continuity between these texts: he remains a trusted figure, a bearer of divine insight, and a bridge between heaven and earth.

What Jubilees adds to the story is structure. It draws boundaries—temporal, moral, legal. It tells the reader not only what happened but when and why, and what should be learned from it. In doing so, it transforms the myth into law, and the cosmic rebellion into a cautionary tale that reinforces the centrality of obedience and the consequences of crossing divine limits. For readers of the Book of Giants, Jubilees provides important context. It shows how the same tradition that gave rise to the fragmented and visionary Book of Giants could also be absorbed into a text that emphasizes order, law, and covenant. The story of the Watchers and the Giants was not only retold—it was disciplined, dated, and made part of a sacred chronology. This reinforces the idea that the myth was never marginal. It was debated, interpreted, and reshaped to meet the needs of different communities and theological frameworks.

In the world of Jubilees, there is no place for ambiguity or pity. The Watchers sinned. The giants corrupted the earth. The flood came. What remains is a lesson, set in stone: divine boundaries exist for a reason, and violating them has consequences that extend far beyond the present generation. That clarity, though less poetic than other apocryphal works, gives Jubilees its enduring authority—and confirms the central importance of the myth it so firmly condemns.

THE BOOK OF GIANTS

Genesis Apocryphon (1Q20)

The Genesis Apocryphon, one of the most intriguing scrolls discovered among the Dead Sea Scrolls at Qumran, offers a unique retelling of stories from the early chapters of Genesis. Though heavily damaged and fragmentary, the text provides a narrative expansion of familiar figures—particularly Lamech, Noah, and Abraham—while interweaving dream sequences, divine visitations, and reinterpretations of known events. Among these is a thematic and symbolic echo of the Book of Giants, most notably through shared motifs of dreams, floods, and the mysterious presence of Enoch.

Composed in Aramaic and dating from the late Second Temple period, the Genesis Apocryphon is not a visionary or apocalyptic text in the style of 1 Enoch, but it nonetheless shares several narrative and theological concerns. It brings the characters of Genesis into a more intimate and dramatic light, sometimes amplifying their inner thoughts and private fears. In one of the most striking surviving episodes, Lamech becomes troubled by the appearance of his newborn son, Noah. His concern is not only paternal—it is cosmic. The child's unusual appearance leads Lamech to question whether the child is of human or divine origin, and whether his wife might have conceived through one of the "holy ones." This directly recalls the Watchers myth, where angelic beings descend and produce hybrid offspring.

Lamech, unsure of what to believe, seeks out his father Methuselah, who in turn turns to Enoch for an answer. Enoch, now dwelling with the holy ones, confirms that Noah is indeed Lamech's son and that his birth is pure and part of a divine plan. In this exchange, Enoch functions in the same role he holds in the Book of Giants: the ultimate interpreter, the one whose insight is trusted when the natural order is in doubt. His words restore order and certainty, distinguishing the legitimate child from the cursed offspring of the Watchers. It is an affirmation of purity in a world overshadowed by the memory of transgression. This episode, though brief, reveals how the myth of the Watchers and their illicit unions lingered just beneath the surface of other sacred narratives. Even in a text that does not focus directly on the giants or the fallen angels, their legacy affects the way people understand signs, birth, and divine will. The fear of unnatural progeny, the anxiety around cosmic boundaries being crossed, and the role of dreams in revealing hidden truths all mirror the emotional and symbolic weight carried in the Book of Giants.

The Genesis Apocryphon also shares an emphasis on dreams and divine revelations. In the story of Abraham, dreams serve as warnings and sources of direction. God's will is communicated not just through prophecy or law, but through symbolic visions that must be interpreted. This reinforces a broader cultural pattern in which dreams are not private or subjective experiences, but structured messages that demand decoding—often by someone specially appointed, like Enoch. In the Book of Giants, the giants are tormented by their own dreams and must seek out Enoch to understand their fate. The Genesis Apocryphon, although more focused on patriarchal figures, follows this same model of dream-as-message, interpreter-as-mediator.

Another point of connection lies in the flood motif. While the Genesis Apocryphon does not provide a complete account of the deluge, the surviving fragments show a strong emphasis on the coming destruction and the unique role of Noah as one who is chosen to survive. The flood looms as divine response to corruption, a cleansing of the earth to restore order. This mirrors the function of the flood in the Book of Giants—not just as a historical event, but as the divine answer to a cosmic imbalance brought about by the existence of the giants.

Although the Genesis Apocryphon is less explicit in its references to the fallen angels, its narrative is haunted by the same themes: questions of lineage, signs of judgment, and the need for divine clarity. Enoch's brief appearance is enough to affirm his ongoing authority within the broader Enochic tradition. Even outside of the overtly apocalyptic texts, his voice continues to carry weight, acting as the anchor that holds conflicting realities together.

For readers of the Book of Giants, the Genesis Apocryphon offers a quieter, more intimate reflection of the same cosmic story. It reveals how the mythology of the Watchers seeped into other sacred retellings—not always with full explanation, but with unmistakable traces. It also shows how Enoch's presence persisted not only as a prophet of doom, but as a voice of reassurance when heaven and earth seemed most unstable.

APPENDIX 2

The Second Book of Enoch (2 Enoch)

The Second Book of Enoch, also known as Slavonic Enoch, presents one of the most elaborate portrayals of Enoch's journey into the heavens. Likely composed between the 1st century BCE and 1st century CE, this text survives primarily in Old Church Slavonic and reflects a sophisticated development of earlier Enochic traditions. While it shares some features with 1 Enoch, its focus is distinct: it emphasizes Enoch's personal transformation, his passage through multiple layers of heaven, and the deepening of cosmic order through structured revelations. For readers of the Book of Giants, 2 Enoch offers essential background on the elevation of Enoch from righteous man to quasi-angelic being, and on the expanding architecture of divine reality.

The text opens with Enoch being taken by two radiant men—interpreted as angelic guides—who lead him upward through the various heavens. As he ascends, he encounters increasing levels of holiness and complexity, each with specific angelic beings, purposes, and structures. From the first heaven, where atmospheric phenomena are explained, to the seventh, where the Lord resides surrounded by fiery seraphim and the ineffable light, Enoch's journey is one of increasing revelation and transformation. He is not simply visiting—he is being changed. By the end of the narrative, Enoch is clothed in glory, anointed with oil, and given the appearance and rank of one of the heavenly ones. This process anticipates his later transformation into the archangel Metatron in 3 Enoch. In contrast to the fragmentary and emotionally charged voices of the Book of Giants, where Enoch acts primarily as an interpreter and messenger of judgment, 2 Enoch presents him as a figure of ultimate authority—both recipient and transmitter of hidden knowledge. He records everything he sees in books and passes this knowledge on to his sons, ensuring that what was once hidden is now part of the righteous tradition. This elevation of Enoch's status helps explain why, in the Book of Giants, even beings like Mahway and Ohya instinctively trust him: his authority is not just moral, but cosmological. He has seen the totality of creation.

The cosmology of 2 Enoch is rich and layered. It introduces detailed classifications of angels, their functions, and their realms of influence. It also delves into the origins of light and darkness, the purpose of time, the measure of the universe, and the balance between mercy and justice. All of this builds a coherent vision of the cosmos as highly ordered and purposeful, in contrast to the chaotic world the Watchers and their offspring have brought into being. The rebellion of the Watchers, although not the main subject of 2 Enoch, is situated within this framework of divine order: the idea that there is a proper place for each being and a limit that must not be crossed.

One of the most significant thematic overlaps between 2 Enoch and the Book of Giants lies in their shared concern with judgment and divine boundaries. While 2 Enoch does not retell the story of the Giants explicitly, it is haunted by the same questions: What happens when celestial beings interfere with the earthly realm? What is the consequence of revealing forbidden knowledge? What role does the human-divine mediator play in transmitting truth and warning of judgment? In both texts, Enoch occupies that critical space—not as a destroyer, but as a scribe, a witness, and a guardian of balance.

The tone of 2 Enoch is less catastrophic than that of 1 Enoch or the Book of Giants, but it carries a profound sense of solemnity. Enoch is constantly reminded that the things he sees must be recorded, preserved, and taught, but not always fully revealed. Some knowledge is for the righteous, while other truths remain sealed. This tension—between what is shown and what is withheld—mirrors the fragmented nature of the Book of Giants itself, where meaning often lies in what is suggested rather than what is stated. Moreover, 2 Enoch reflects a transitional period in Jewish thought, one in which visionary experiences were being structured into broader theological systems. The elevation of Enoch and the expansion of angelology serve to reinforce a worldview where divine justice is exact, knowledge is stratified, and mediation is necessary. In such a framework, the role of beings like the Watchers and their hybrid children is implicitly condemned—not just morally, but cosmologically. They do not fit within the ordered heavens that Enoch now understands and inhabits.

Enoch offers a vital piece of the puzzle. It shows how the figure of Enoch evolved from a mysterious scribe to a central pillar of cosmological understanding. It also demonstrates how the ideas of hidden wisdom, divine law, and heavenly hierarchy became essential tools for interpreting the fall—not just of angels, but of all who disrupt the order of creation.

Gnostic Echoes: Gospel of Judas & Gospel of Mary

Though written centuries after the Book of Giants and shaped by very different theological frameworks, the Gnostic texts known as the Gospel of Judas and the Gospel of Mary echo many of the same themes found in Enochic literature. These writings, associated with early Christian and Gnostic communities of the 2nd and 3rd centuries CE, are not concerned with giants, Watchers, or floods in any direct sense. Yet beneath their narratives lie shared concerns: secret knowledge, the rebellion of spiritual beings, and the human struggle to understand a divided cosmos.

The Gospel of Judas, discovered in a Coptic manuscript in the 1970s and published in translation in the early 2000s, presents a radically different portrait of Judas Iscariot—not as the betrayer of Christ, but as the disciple who truly understood his master's divine plan. Central to this gospel is the idea that Jesus has come to reveal hidden truths, and that those truths are reserved for the few who can receive them. In a striking section of the text, Jesus describes the flawed creation of the world and the existence of lower spiritual beings—angels and rulers—who resist the true divine order. These rulers, sometimes called archons, bear strong resemblance to the rebellious Watchers of earlier Jewish tradition. They are powerful, celestial, but ultimately corrupted by pride and ignorance.

This vision of the cosmos, divided between a pure, hidden realm and a flawed material world governed by deceptive powers, resonates with the framework found in the Book of Giants. In both, the cosmos is a battleground of knowledge and hierarchy. The Watchers descend and corrupt the earth by revealing secrets not meant for mankind. In the Gospel of Judas, Jesus withholds the full truth from the other disciples because they cannot understand it—and because their attachment to the earthly temple blinds them to the higher realities. Judas alone receives the hidden knowledge, just as Enoch alone is trusted to interpret the dreams of the giants and deliver the verdict of heaven.

The Gospel of Mary, likewise a Gnostic-leaning text, emphasizes inner revelation and spiritual liberation over obedience to external law. In it, Mary Magdalene recounts a vision she received from the risen Christ. When challenged by the male disciples, she asserts her understanding not through authority, but through insight—spiritual clarity that transcends institutional hierarchy. This emphasis on vision, inner truth, and divine knowledge withheld from the many but entrusted to the few mirrors the role of Enoch across the Enochic corpus.

Though the Book of Giants is rooted in a very different religious world, its narrative centers on knowledge that has been wrongly given and must now be corrected. The giants receive dreams but cannot interpret them. The Watchers give secrets that bring destruction. Enoch, the mediator, becomes a channel through which true understanding is restored—not freely, but with solemn weight. Similarly, the Gnostic gospels emphasize that not all knowledge is equal, and not all are ready to receive it. Truth is powerful, but also dangerous. Revelation requires readiness. The failure to understand is not just ignorance—it is a spiritual flaw. Another shared feature is the redefinition of judgment. In the Book of Giants, judgment is inevitable and comes from above, but it is mediated through vision and interpretation. In the Gnostic texts, judgment is internal: those who cling to ignorance remain trapped in the material world; those who embrace insight ascend. While the mechanics differ, the spiritual logic is strikingly similar. The greatest threat is not sin in the traditional sense, but the misuse—or misunderstanding—of knowledge that crosses divine boundaries.

Enoch and Mary, though vastly different figures, serve similar narrative functions. They stand apart. They receive what others cannot. They are tested, questioned, and entrusted with messages that are not meant for the many. Their authority does not come from power or position, but from having seen what lies beyond the visible.

For readers of the Book of Giants, these Gnostic echoes invite reflection on the broader tradition of sacred knowledge—who receives it, who distorts it, and what it means to carry it. They also show that the concerns of the Enochic world did not vanish after the destruction of the Second Temple. Instead, they resurfaced in new forms, in new languages, in communities wrestling with the same spiritual questions: Where is truth found? Who dares to speak it? And what happens when divine secrets enter a world not ready to receive them?

A Myth That Endures

The Book of Giants occupies a strange place in the landscape of apocryphal literature—fragmentary, elusive, and yet foundational. Unlike more polished or preserved texts, it survives only in pieces, scattered across different languages and cultures. And yet, those pieces reveal a narrative that continues to resonate across centuries: a story of celestial rebellion, human corruption, prophetic visions, and the tension between hidden knowledge and divine justice.

What makes this text particularly striking is how its themes ripple outward into other writings, even when it is not explicitly named. From the rigid structure of Jubilees to the symbolic visions of Gnostic gospels, echoes of the Book of Giants can be found in places both expected and surprising. Some texts tame its myth, placing it within legal or liturgical order. Others adapt it into new metaphysical frameworks, turning giants into spiritual symbols or cosmic metaphors. In both cases, the core elements remain recognizable: beings who transgress, knowledge that disrupts, and a world seeking balance.

In this web of apocalyptic memory, Enoch stands as the connecting thread. He is the one figure who appears across traditions without losing his distinct voice. Whether as heavenly scribe, prophetic messenger, or exalted mediator, Enoch represents the capacity to hold knowledge without being corrupted by it. His presence affirms that revelation is possible, but it is never casual. It comes with responsibility, with risk, and with the need for discernment.

The Book of Giants may be incomplete, but its role is not minor. It speaks for a worldview that saw the cosmos as structured yet vulnerable, where boundaries mattered and where crossing them came at great cost. It reminds us that ancient authors were not only storytellers but interpreters of a broken world—offering visions not just of destruction, but of meaning. And even in silence, even in fragments, their voices still reach us.

www.ingramcontent.com/pod-product-compliance
Lightning Source LLC
Chambersburg PA
CBHW071900070526
44583CB00016B/1773